Unlocking the Scriptures for You

MARK

Paul R. McReynolds

STANDARD
BIBLE STUDIES

STANDARD PUBLISHING
Cincinnati, Ohio   11-40102

Unless otherwise noted, all other Scripture quotations are from the *Holy Bible: New International Version,* © 1973, 1978, 1984 by the International Bible Society. Used by permission of Zondervan Bible Publishers and the International Bible Society.

Sharing the thoughts of his own heart, the author may express views not entirely consistent with those of the publisher.

Library of Congress Cataloging in Publication Data:

McReynolds, Paul R., 1936-
  Mark / by Paul R. McReynolds.
  p. cm. —(Standard Bible studies)
  Bibliography: p.
ISBN 0-87403-162-1 :
1. Bible. N.T. Mark—Commentaries. I. Title. II. Series.
BS2585.M43   1989   226'.307—dc   1989-4137

                                                    CIP

Dedicated to Madeline, who devoted many hours editing my ramblings into a coherent text.

CONTENTS

PREFACE

This preface contains important information that the reader of the commentary needs to understand my work concerning the Gospel of Mark. While some of the material provides brief but necessary background information, the rest of the material gives my approach to the text.

John Mark, a follower of both Paul and Peter, is the author. Most of the information he uses to write the book comes from the apostle Peter. The book was written sometime between A.D. 65-75. I prefer a date shortly after 70 (the fall of Jerusalem). Mark writes to Christians (probably in Rome) who have been and are currently suffering persecution from Roman authorities, partly as a carry-over from Nero's time and partly as a result of the Jewish rebellion in Palestine. Christians for some time were viewed by the Romans as a Jewish sect.

The book was written to be read orally to a Christian audience in order to strengthen them in their commitment to Jesus Christ, the Son of God. This important purpose guides Mark in his selection and description of events. The accuracy of the book is assured by the primary resource (Peter) and, of course, by the inspiration of God's Spirit.

This commentary makes little use of Gospel parallels since Mark's audience understood what he wrote without using parallels. Mark was likely the first Gospel writer. If so, then it is impossible to make deductions from his addition or subtraction of materials that we know occur in the other Gospels. Mark's text was meant to be read and understood on its own, and the current readers should respect the author's intention.

This commentary is written for a general church audience and is therefore without technical notes. For those who wish to pursue any of the text further with othery resources, I would recommend especially the two commentaries by Lane and Cranfield. The Rhodes-Michie book provides an excellent understanding for the unique audience-story narrative form of Mark.

Frequently, New Testament quotations that appear here are my own translations from the Greek text. These will be marked "A.T." (that is, Author's Translation). The Scripture quotations are generally from the New International Version, in keeping with the Publisher's style for this series. Other versions, when cited, will be marked.

The reader will notice quickly a somewhat different vocabulary. I have studiously attempted to avoid as much religious jargon as possible so that others who are not acquainted with the inside connotations of traditional Christian vocabulary can also understand the commentary. I have also found in my teaching that changing the vocabulary helps many longtime Christians to gain new insights to some familiar Christian concepts.

I have tried to emphasize that the text of Mark that was written in A.D. 65-75 is really God's Word. We should not use Mark then to reconstruct Jesus' life and teachings in A.D 30-33. The text of Mark was written for a Christian church in the middle of persecution to give it assurance that the One they followed was indeed the Son of God. Thus, Mark needs to be interpreted in the light of what he is trying to say in A.D. 65-75, although he writes about events that happened in A.D. 30-33. In other words, Mark has already interpreted by inspiration the events of A.D. 30-33; so our task is to understand this interpretation in the light of A.D. 65-75 in order that we make appropriate applications to our own time.

We all know that Jesus taught prior to His death, burial, and resurrection. However, it is His death, burial, and resurrection that make His teaching valuable. Thus we, like Mark's audience, understand all Jesus' teachings in the light of His death, burial, and resurrection while Jesus' audience did not know the "rest of the story." Again this emphasizes Mark's inspired interpretation in A.D. 65-75 of Jesus' life and teachings. So we must understand what Mark is trying to teach by his selection, description, and arrangement of events in Jesus' life. He is not simply enumerating the simple facts regarding Jesus' life. The important question always is, "What does Mark want his readers to know and/or to do because of the events about which he is writing?" We, in turn, are also readers of his book and we must constantly ask ourselves that same question.

Finally it must be said that this commentary is not at all meant to be a substitute for reading the text of Mark. The text of Mark is not reproduced in the commentary because I want the reader to read and reread the text. Ideally, the reader should read and study the text, then investigate commentaries, and finally but always return to the text (2 Timothy 3:16-18).

The following outline of Mark's Gospel is offered to help the reader understand what I believe to be Mark's own arrangement of the text. It is then, the pattern I have followed in writing this commentary. The reader will notice the similarity between this outline and the table of contents for this work. The latter is greatly condensed, however, and the reader is well advised to notice this outline in order to understand the flow of thought both in Mark's Gospel and in this work. The number in brackets next to each section cited on the outline indicate the page number where the comments on that section begins.

Jesus Christ Is the Son of God (Mark 1:1) [17]

I. The Evident Power and Authority of Jesus, the Son of God (Mark 1:2—8:26) [19]

A. The Urgency of Jesus' Mission (Mark 1:2-20) [21]
1. Jesus' Preparer (Mark 1:2-8) [21]
2. God's approval of Jesus' immersion (Mark 1:9-11) [22]
3. Pressures in the desert (Mark 1:12, 13) [22]
4. Jesus' announcement (Mark 1:14, 15) [23]
5. Jesus' call to follow (Mark 1:16-20) [24]

B. Jesus' Power and Authority Are Demonstrated (Mark 1:21-8:26) [25]
1. Through healings (Mark 1:21-45) [25]
   a. Of demon possessed people (Mark 1:21-28) [25]
   b. Of Peter's mother-in-law (Mark 1:29-31) [26]
   c. Of many (Mark 1:32-39) [27]
   d. Of a leper (Mark 1:40-45) [28]
2. Through controversies (Mark 2:1-28) [31]
   a. Over healing on the Sabbath (Mark 2:1-12) [31]
   b. Over association with sinners (Mark 2:13-17) [32]
   c. Over fastings (Mark 2:18-22) [34]
   d. Over working on the Sabbath (Mark 2:23-28) [35]
3. Through expansion of His service (Mark 3:1-35) [37]
   a. By further healing on the Sabbath (Mark 3:1-6) [37]
   b. By the calling of His learners (Mark 3:7-19) [38]
   c. By opposition of family, friends and scribe (Mark 3:20-35) [40]
4. Through parallel story teaching (Mark 4:1-34) [45]
   a. Story of seed and soil (Mark 4:1-9, 14-20) [45]
   b. The understanding of stories (Mark 4:10-13, 33, 34) [47]
   c. Be careful listeners (Mark 4:21-25) [48]
   d. The seed stories (Mark 4:26-32) [49]
5. Through a nature miracle (Mark 4:35-41) [50]
6. Through further healings (Mark 5:1-43) [53]
   a. A man possessed by many demons (Mark 5:1-20) [53]

13

C. Third Prediction of His Death and the Reaction (Mark 10:32-52) [114]
   1. Jesus teaches about His death (Mark 10:32-34) [114]
   2. Jesus teaches servanthood (Mark 10:35-45) [115]
      a. To James and John (Mark 10:35-40) [115]
      b. To the other learners (Mark 10:41-45) [116]
   3. The healing of blind Bartimaeus (Mark 10:46-52) [117]

III. **Jesus Demonstrates the True Nature and Purpose of His Sonship (Mark 11:1—16:8) [121]**

A. In Teaching and Conflict at Jerusalem (Mark 11:1—13:37) [123]
   1. Messianic entrance to Jerusalem (Mark 11:1-11) [123]
   2. Fig tree (Mark 11:12-14) [125]
   3. Cleaning the temple (Mark 11:15-19) [126]
   4. The fig tree and prayer (Mark 11:20-26) [126]
   5. Questions (Mark 11:27—13:31) [129]
      a. The question about authority (Mark 11:27-33) [129]
      b. The vineyard parallel story (Mark 12:1-12) [130]
      c. The question about taxes (Mark 12:13-17) [131]
      d. The question about marriage (Mark 12:18-27) [134]
      e. The question about the greatest command (Mark 12:28-34) [136]
      f. Jesus questions the scribes' hypocrisy (Mark 12:35-44) [138]
      g. Learners question the temple destruction (Mark 13:1-31) [144]

B. In Preparation for Death (Mark 14:1-42) [155]
   1. The death plot (Mark 14:1-2) [155]
   2. Anointing for burial (Mark 14:3-9) [156]
   3. Judas begins his betrayal (Mark 14:10, 11) [158]
   4. Passover celebration (Mark 14:12-25) [158]
   5. Jesus predicts denial and desertions (Mark 14:26-31) [164]
   6. Jesus prays while learners sleep (Mark 14:32-42) [165]

C. In Trial and Crucifixion (Mark 14:43—15:47) [166]

INTRODUCTION

Jesus Christ Is the Son of God

Mark 1:1

The unique proclamation that begins Mark's Gospel is actually the title of his book. Mark's Gospel begins neither with a genealogy nor the birth of Jesus, as the other Synoptic Gospel narratives do, but with the prophecy by Isaiah and Malachi that Jesus will be preceded by a voice shouting in the desert. Mark shows little interest in Jesus' early life. In fact, he mentions John the Baptist, Jesus' immersion, His desert temptations, and His opening announcement only briefly. The ministry of Jesus begins for Mark when Jesus selects His first followers, Peter and John.

The expression *gospel* in Mark's title is more appropriately translated "good news." Mark uses this word eight times, six times as a reference to Jesus' teaching without further indication of the word's content. The content is only explicit in Mark 1:14. In the title, the good news is about Jesus Christ. This is meant as an announcement. In early secular literature, the word meant joyful news that either an Emperor was born or that he had been enthroned. The word in the Old Testament is most often related to the future time deliverance by God. Do we need good news today? Read the the front page of your daily paper if you have any doubts. The news about Jesus Christ should be good news to anyone who has never heard about Him, but in reality it is only good news if that person accepts Jesus as the Christ. If Jesus is rejected, then bad news will have to be faced at the end of the person's life.

One aspect of good news is that it impels us to act. Who can resist spreading good news? When my grandchildren were born, I told all my associates at the college where I teach—and everyone else I met! Is being a Christian meaningful to you? Do you have good news? Do you have something to share? Since it really is good news, you naturally want to pass it on to others. The gospel

17

is good news of the highest theological significance. Jesus is the Christ, the Son of God! What exciting news to tell!

The full title, Jesus Christ, occurs only once in Mark, and in this first verse. The expression *Son of God,* though it is not found in some of the earliest manuscripts, is so expressive of the major theme of Mark that there is little doubt that it is a part of the original text. Jesus is declared to be the Son of God by His Father in Mark 1:11 and 9:7, by demons in Mark 3:11 and 5:7, and finally by the Roman centurion in Mark 15:39. To say that Jesus is the Son of God may not really be that unique since we are all indeed sons of God. However, Jesus is unique as Son of God since God gave birth to Him through the Holy Spirit. This is the reason John refers to Jesus as the only begotten Son of God. God in a unique way existed in Him (Colossians 1:19) and was in Christ reconciling the world to himself (2 Corinthians 5:19). Thus, we do not need to think of Jesus as a son who is subordinate to His Father as you and I are to our fathers, because this expression really means that He and the Father are one and the same.

Part One

The Evident Power and Authority of Jesus, the Son of God

Mark 1:2—8:30

CHAPTER ONE

The Beginning

Mark 1:2-45

The Urgency of Jesus' Mission (1:2-20)

Jesus' Preparer (2-8)

The early church's Scripture was what we now call the Old Testament; so naturally Mark begins his account of Jesus by quoting two prophets. He quotes Malachi 3:1 first, which concerns the judgment on Israel and the need for a savior. Second, he quotes Isaiah 40:3, which promises deliverance from captivity. The appearance, then, of John the Immerser has been foreseen by the prophets, who pictured him as the one who precedes both judgment and deliverance. This appearance parallels Jesus' appearance as the good news because rejection of the good news means bad news for those who reject it—there is judgment as well as deliverance. John shows himself to be in the legitimate line of the prophets by his living place (a desert) and by his particular food and clothing. (See 2 Kings 1:8; Zechariah 13:4.)

John's announcement had three parts: first, John announced an immersion of repentance for the forgiveness of sins. Many people came out to see and hear him and were convinced enough to be immersed while confessing their sins. Actually, these people who acknowledged their sins were then ready for the coming of the Lord, or deliverer, who was announced by John. The second part of John's announcement was that one even stronger than John was coming. John knew that he was not even worthy to untie this person's sandals, an act that was usually performed by slaves. The third part of John's announcement was that although he immersed people into water, the stronger one would immerse His followers into the Holy Spirit. Mark's audience would have fully understood what John meant because they knew that the age of the church was also the age of the Holy Spirit, and that immersion into water and immersion into the Spirit were one concept for their Christian community.

21

Mark's writing style condenses the ministry of John and Jesus' immersion and temptations because he wants to convey the urgency of Jesus' mission. Mark also wants to proceed quickly to the active part of Jesus' ministry. Mark's urgency is indicated in his first chapter by the repeated choice of the word *immediately.*

God's Approval of Jesus' Immersion (9-11)

Mark moves quickly through this part of his story, and even omits Jesus' discussion with John. Mark simply says that Jesus was immersed by John, and then he records the immediate vision Jesus has when the Spirit comes down as a dove and a voice declares from Heaven that Jesus is the loved Son of God with whom God is well pleased. Mark has tied the immersion Jesus will perform ("He will baptize you with the Holy Spirit"; Mark 1:8) to the fact that the Spirit also comes to Jesus at His immersion by John (Mark 1:10). This is all preparation for the service of Jesus. The purpose of Jesus' immersion is clear in John's Gospel when John the immerser says, "I myself did not know Him; but He who sent me to immerse with water said to me, 'He on whom you see the Spirit descend and remain, this is he who immerses with the Holy Spirit.' And I have seen and have borne witness that this is the Son of God" (John 1:33, 34, A.T.) This passage also affirms the title of Mark's Gospel; that is, Jesus is the Son of God. This title will be affirmed several more times by various individuals throughout Mark's text.

Most of us wonder why it was necessary for Jesus to be immersed, especially when we connect immersion with the forgiveness of sins. Perhaps Jesus himself wondered, but He obeyed, and His obedience was voluntary. His voluntary obedience enabled God's declaration that Jesus was His Son and that He was pleased with Him. It is also true for us that we gain His approval when we obey Him voluntarily. Jesus faced mockery at the end of His life. He died voluntarily by denying His will but yielding to the will of His Father. He knew that His voluntary obedience brought not only mockery and death, but also His resurrection.

Pressures in the Desert (12, 13)

After the strong affirmation of God's approval, Jesus is sent into the desert by the Spirit, where He is pressured by Satan, the adversary, for forty days. After we are immersed into Christ, we also face pressure from old friends and old ways. The high mountains of good experiences with God are often followed by the bleak desert valleys of pressures where we must face ourselves and live out our commitment. However, God's Spirit was with Jesus not only in His immersion, but also when the pressures came. Happily, this is also true for us.

Note the five characters who play a part in the drama of this brief section. The Spirit and the angels are on one side, Satan and the wild beasts are on the other, and Jesus is alone and in the middle. Most of our own pressures come when we are in the middle between right and wrong. But not all pressures come from Satan. James reminds us that we are often pressured by our own selfish desires (James 1:14, 15). Jesus reminds us that sometimes we are pressured by other people (Mark 12:15). Pressures, like the announcement of the good news, can produce either judgment and death or deliverance and growth. To submit to pressures is to bring sin and then death; to overcome pressures brings strength and life. Jesus came through the pressures ready to begin His public service.

Jesus' Announcement (14, 15)

Mark briefly describes the basic message of Jesus again. After John's imprisonment, Jesus comes to Galilee and publicly announces the good news from God. This announcement has two declarations and two commands.

> The season is right. The kingdom of God has neared.
> Change your mind. Trust in the good news (Mark 1:15, A.T.).

Jesus directs the first two declarations to His audience. They need to hear that what everyone has been waiting for and wanting is about to begin. The old age is finished; the new age is approaching. To say that the kingdom of God has neared makes sense to Jesus' audience, but Mark's audience needs to understand that the kingdom of God has, in fact, come in the person of Jesus, His actions on the cross, and God's action in the resurrection. The kingdom of God means the reign of God or the sovereignty of God in the lives of His people. Jesus is the kingdom and the kingdom is Jesus. The kingdom is not physical as many in Jesus' audience thought it would be, but it is nonetheless real for the person who allows the risen Savior to be king in his or her life.

Jesus' good news is the announcement about the kingdom's nearness and the command to change your mind and trust in the good news. For Mark's audience, and for us, the announcement is not about something to come but about the establishment of the kingdom in the death and resurrection of Jesus. The response to the announcement for Jesus' audience and for us, however, is the same. We are to change our minds and trust the good news. The critical difference between Jesus' announcement and ours is that while Jesus announced the good news of the coming kingdom, we proclaim Jesus as the good news.

These verses also give us the first indication of the authority of Jesus, which is one of Mark's major themes. Jesus not only has the authority to make an important announcement about the kingdom, but He also can command obedience as a logical response to His announcement.

Jesus' Call to Follow (16-20)

Because Mark's style is so brief, there is an impression that this is the first time that Jesus has talked to these men. The other Gospels, however, make it clear that Jesus had talked with them on other occasions. (See Luke 5:1-11 and John 1:35-42.) Jesus' call to them really is the culmination of previous teaching sessions. It is at this point, however, that Jesus asks these men to come with Him and learn more. The analogy concerning fishers of men is an analogy of judgment according to the Old Testament references (Jeremiah 16:16; Ezekiel 29:4; Amos 4:2; Habakkuk 1:14-17). The decision one makes to follow Jesus is a decision for life; a decision not to follow Jesus is a decision for judgment. In one sense, Jesus "catches" followers as others catch fish, but with His authoritative word instead of a net or hook. Jesus intends to teach His followers so that they, in turn, can catch others with His authoritative words.

James, John, Simon, and Andrew followed Jesus through trust. They certainly did not understand everything, but they were willing to follow. They were so willing to follow that when the invitation (command) came, they literally left everything behind and followed. Simon and Andrew were in the middle of throwing a fishing net, while James and John were mending nets in their boat with their father and the hired hands. All these men left behind what they were doing and followed Jesus. When Jesus calls, we must act. The objective of following Jesus is to serve.

Put another way, serving Jesus requires us to "fish" for more followers.

Jesus' relationship with His followers has often been likened to that of a rabbi and his disciples. But there are several distinctions that should be made. Normally, a disciple seeks and finds a rabbi. Jesus, on the other hand, seeks and calls His own followers. Learners debated with, served, and even tried to replace the rabbi. Jesus, however, never debated with His followers, and He ultimately served them far more than they ever could have served Him.

What does God expect of those who follow Him? Trusting obedience, perhaps changes in occupation and family relations, and a faithful witness. The story of the calling of these learners is a model for Mark's audience and for us. It shows us how we who call ourselves learners of Christ should obey and trust.

Jesus' Power and Authority
Are Demonstrated Through Healings (1:21-45)

After the introduction of Jesus, Mark simply relates one event after another in order to demonstrate Jesus' authority. His authority is demonstrated over illness, demons, and nature. It is seen in controversies with Pharisees and in the selection of Jesus' followers. These events occupy Mark's narrative from this point to Mark 8:26. The turning point of the gospel is at Mark 8:27, when Peter professes his trust in Jesus as the Christ.

Demon-possessed People (21-28)

Mark's telling of the events is characteristically brief. This event has three main characters: the audience, the unclean spirit, and Jesus. The audience includes the followers that Jesus has just called to become fishers of men. The fishermen's reaction is the most important part of Mark's account. They are amazed at the onset by the authority of Jesus' teaching style. They are amazed again at His authority when He commands the unclean spirit to come out of the man and when the unclean spirit immediately obeys.

The unclean spirit recognizes Jesus, just as Jesus recognizes the unclean spirit. Jesus and the unclean spirit are true opposites, and they both know this. Jesus is the "Holy One of God" (Mark 1:24), and the spirit is unclean, the opposite of "holy." Jesus' conflict shown in the Gospel of Mark is too often seen only as a conflict between himself and the Pharisees or scribes, but this event illustrates not only a worldly conflict, but also a cosmic conflict between Jesus and the forces of evil that are represented by the unclean spirit. Jesus is the ultimate victor because the unclean spirit knows that Jesus has the ability to destroy him. The unclean spirit must recognize Jesus' authority as the Son of God.

Mark does not record much dialogue in this section. The author states that the unclean spirit recognizes Jesus and protests. Jesus then gives two simple commands: "Be quiet" (literally, "Be silent"), and, "Come out of him." Jesus says, "Be silent," because He does not want the unclean spirit to announce Jesus' real identity, and He also knows that when the spirit does come out, he will emerge with a shout. The obedience of the unclean spirit to the commands of Jesus again demonstrates Jesus' authority.

Jesus' authority is also demonstrated by His teaching. His teaching content is impressive, but His presentation also exudes authority. Jesus taught with immediate self-authenticating authority. The scribes taught with the authority of tradition, relying on what others had already said. Jesus' teaching recalled the categorical demand of the prophets rather than the chain of scribal tradition. Mark's Gospel stresses the fact that Jesus taught, but reports very little content of Jesus' teaching—unlike Matthew and Luke.

Mark emphasizes the audience's amazement at Jesus' teaching and healing. He wants to demonstrate the authority of Jesus as the Holy One of God to his audience and to us. Mark wants his church to know that Jesus had authority and that even when men (even His followers) did not recognize it, demons did. Demons recognized and obeyed Jesus. Ought we, who claim to be on His side, do less?

Peter's Mother-in-law (29-31)

The urgency and priority of Jesus' service is shown by Mark's use of the word *immediately* and, in this section, by the description of time. Note that the unclean spirit incident occurs on the Sabbath; the healing of Peter's mother-in-law happens in the afternoon; that evening, the crowds gather for healing; then, before daylight the next morning, Jesus slips away for prayer and then announces a mission to other villages.

This is the first healing in Mark (if we distinguish between throwing out demons and healing diseases). Though brief, it does show a proper response to healing. That response is service. Peter's mother-in-law is healed and immediately begins to serve. (She probably prepares a meal for them.) One of the hard concepts to understand in Mark is why the followers have a constant negative reaction to Jesus' service. In contrast to Jesus' followers, women are seen in a very favorable light in Mark. Peter's mother-in-law, the widow in Mark 12:41f, the woman who anoints Jesus in Mark 14:3f, and the women at the tomb all are treated favorably by Mark, in contrast to the way he shows the hardness of Jesus' followers—all men.

Many (32-39)

Mark 1:32-34 forms a summary of both healing and throwing out of demons. Jesus will not let the demons testify concerning Him. Mark indicates that unclean spirits, evil spirits, and demons are synonymous terms. In Mark, these spirits are shown to be responsible for insanity (Mark 5:1-15), epilepsy, sickness, and deafness (Mark 9:14-27), but there are also cases of demon possession without illness (Mark 1:26). Nor are all illnesses in Mark's Gospel due to demons; for example, the previous incident of fever and the next incident concerning the leper.

Today, we know some of the physical causes of diseases such as insanity, epilepsy, and deafness, but the cause of all illness is a corruption of God's perfect creation, which is attributable to evil. What can a sick person today expect from God? Illness is certainly not punishment. Jesus healed many. Illness is not peculiar to certain individuals. Healing is possible both naturally, through our natural bodily defenses and the aid of modern medicine, and through supernatural means that we are not completely able to explain.

Jesus' service was not centered around healing. Jesus often had to leave an area so that He could continue with His teaching when His ability to heal interfered with His mission. The next incident in Mark illustrates this problem.

In order to have some privacy and prayer, Jesus left the town before daybreak and found a deserted place. The press of the people and His followers was constant, but Jesus' need for quiet prayer was vital. Jesus also draws away for prayer in Mark 6:46 and 14:32. If prayer was so important for the Son of God, what does that say about our need for private prayer? This incident really focuses on Jesus' purpose for service. While Jesus could and did throw out demons, He knew this was only one way to demonstrate His authority in order that people would pay attention to His announcement of the good news.

When Simon and the followers find Jesus, they apparently want Him to return to Capernaum and teach and heal the people there. Jesus states His purpose: He must go to other towns and announce. Jesus goes throughout Galilee with His followers preaching, but also throwing out demons. Jesus' authority in teaching and in actions demonstrate Him as the Son of God to His audience, to Mark's church, and to you and me.

A Leper (40-45)

Repetition is a good teaching tool, and Mark knows this. He recounts events in Jesus' life that repeat the same basic teaching about Jesus' authority. For example, a leper comes to Jesus, kneels, and asks to be healed. The leper says, "If you want, you are able to clean me." Jesus replies, "I want. Be clean!" (Mark 1:40, 41, A.T.). Jesus has an exact response to the leper's request, as shown below:

The Leper: "If you **want,** you are able to **clean** me."
Jesus: "I **want.** Be **clean.**"

The leper recognizes Jesus' ability; his only question is whether Jesus wants to exercise His authority. The leper demonstrates a great amount of faith. Not only does he (a leper, an untouchable) dare to approach Jesus, but his only question concerns not Jesus' ability to heal, but whether He wishes to do so.

This incident also shows the human side of Jesus' emotions. Jesus sees the man with his affliction and feels compassion rather than revulsion. He reaches out and touches the untouchable one. The word *leprosy* in Biblical times was a term used to indicate skin diseases. Everyone commonly avoided contact with leprous people because they were afraid their disease was contagious. Leprosy was a condition that could not be hidden. Jesus' emotional response is compassionate, His physical response is to touch the man's sores in order to heal them. When He sends the man away, the text says that Jesus sternly charged him not to discuss the incident. The expression *sternly charged* occurs only five times in the New Testament. It is used four times in describing how Jesus spoke to someone. The term comes from classical Greek vocabulary and means "snorting like a horse." Mark uses it to indicate Jesus' deep feelings of frustration, for while He orders the man not to tell, He apparently knows the man will blurt out what happened, and then Jesus will again be besieged by the crowds. And this is precisely what happens.

Mark records that most of Jesus' demands for silence are frustrated. Jesus tells the demon-possessed man to be quiet, but only after he acknowledges Jesus as the Holy One of God. Jesus asks this man not to tell anyone; but the man tells his story over and over and even more people crowd Jesus. This story is a very realistic picture of Jesus' frustration. Jesus wants to teach about the kingdom of God, but the people want to be healed. He initially leaves Capernaum to teach in other villages (Mark 1:38) because the crowd is filled with people who desire healing. The leper desires healing and Jesus heals; the man tells everyone despite Jesus' stern warning, with the result that Jesus cannot travel in any city openly but has to stay in the countryside to avoid being mobbed. The people come from everywhere and find Jesus, even when He stays in the countryside. Jesus' popularity for healing prevents His teaching message from being heard. Teaching and healing are at cross purposes. Why did the leper disobey Jesus? Jesus wanted him not to tell anyone and to make appropriate sacrifices because of his healing. Jesus did what the man wanted and healed him, but the man does not do what Jesus wants. Yet how can the man be quiet about his stunning healing? Why does Mark include this story of disobedience? Perhaps because Mark wants us to understand that this man was told not to tell and he felt compelled to tell everyone, and we are told to tell our good news and we will not!

CHAPTER TWO

Controversies

Mark 2:1-28

Mark has brought together five events here that illustrate the kinds of controversy Jesus has with the Pharisees and their scribes. Scribes are professional teachers and interpreters of the Mosaic law in addition to being those who write information down for others. The controversies are precipitated by Jesus and His learners. As the first controversy ends, people are amazed; as the last controversy ends, people are hatching a plot to destroy Jesus. The three middle events all end with Jesus' making significant pronouncements that upset the fixed theological ideas of the Pharisees. Jesus approaches these controversies with human concern, but also with His authority and correct teaching.

Healing on the Sabbath (2:1-12)

Jesus is still being pressed by large crowds, so much that a paralyzed man who wants to be healed cannot reach Jesus. The man's companions tear tiles from the roof and dig through in order to lower their sick friend down to Jesus. Mark comments that Jesus saw their trust. But what did Jesus really see? He saw physical actions that indicated sincere trust. Although we are instructed to walk by trust and not by sight, it is understood that our trust must also be seen. All of these men's actions were impressive evidence of their trust.

Jesus' response to their trust was to pronounce forgiveness of the paralyzed man's sins. From this declaration, we must assume there is some connection between sin and sickness in this incident. Certainly not all sickness is a direct result of sin, but sin brought sickness and death into the world. God through Christ is healing and forgiving while He drives sin out of the world.

Another reason for the statement about sin in this section is that Jesus is concerned about the whole person, that is, both body

31

and soul (healing and forgiveness). We readily recognize one need but not the other. Note the various concerns of the people present at this event. Jesus is concerned about soul and body; the four men and their paralyzed friend are concerned about his health, and the scribes are concerned about a theological point.

Jesus' pronouncement about the forgiveness of the man's sins catches us all off guard. Note that it is a statement of fact. Jesus does not say, "I forgive your sins," but, "Your sins are forgiven." The scribes take issue with this statement because only God can forgive sins. They accuse Jesus of blasphemy. Jesus replies by asking a rhetorical question that He does not expect them to answer: which is easier, to forgive sins or to heal? For humans, neither is easier. Either is possible for the Son of Man. In fact, Jesus does both.

The expression *Son of Man* is Jesus' self-identification. In some cases in the New Testament, this phrase is equivalent to the pronoun *I*. It is Jesus' preferred term for himself because He identifies with man. It is a difficult phrase for Jesus' opponents because it raises the issue of God in flesh. They consider the idea scandalous. They cannot understand it. They do not understand Jesus' pronouncement of forgiveness, and they are unwilling to allow God to operate in their midst. They are not willing to admit that Jesus has authority to forgive sins and to heal.

Association With Sinners (2:13-17)

The call to Levi, who is most often identified with the book of Matthew, is as brief as Mark's passage about Jesus' calls to the fishermen. Jesus says, "Follow me," and Levi leaves his job and follows. It should be noted that Levi was not as able to go back to his tax-collecting job as the fishermen were to their nets.

Levi collected toll or customs taxes on all goods transported to Galilee from the Decapolis, Syria, or Judea for Herod Antipas, the Tetrarch of Galilee. Jewish tax collectors were considered traitors by the Pharisees. The fact that Jesus called a Jewish tax collector to be a close follower thus tainted Jesus and the rest of His followers in the Pharisees' eyes. Most Jews would consider all of them suspect, and probably outcasts through association. This paragraph sets the stage for the various controversies that follow.

Who exactly was the host of this dinner is not clear from Mark's account. He merely records it was at Levi's (Matthew's) house. Luke, however, says clearly that Levi was the host (Luke

5:29). Levi had invited his friends to meet Jesus. Levi's friends, of course, were probably fellow tax collectors and others who were commonly called "sinners." These "sinners" were the "Am har aretz" in Aramaic, or the "people of the land." These people were the majority of the Jews who did not follow the Pharisaic interpretations of the law, especially ceremonial cleaning (Mark 7:1f). The fact that they were ceremonially unclean made them sinners. We need to understand that Jesus was in the middle of the most disreputable crowd of Jews that could be gathered together. To speak with these people was bad enough, but actually to sit down and share a meal with them was unthinkable for a practicing Jew. Such a Jew would normally eat only with those who were of "like precious faith." Mark addresses the issue of eating and unclean foods in the seventh chapter and makes it quite clear through Jesus' teaching (and Mark's side comment) that table fellowship is not a matter of clean or unclean hands, clean or unclean foods. In Mark's church, the matter of table fellowship must extend to all those Jesus wants invited, that is, outcasts and others. We must be careful in the church today not only to invite but to welcome those who may be outcasts: these persons need the love and forgiveness that the church offers in Christ's name. It is very easy for us to become modern-day Pharisees by associating only with those of "like precious faith."

Jesus states that He came not for the "right" ones but for the sinners, not for the healthy but for the sick. A current proverb in Jesus' day said, "The well do not need the healer; the sick need the healer."

Jesus is trying to teach the Pharisees, as Mark is trying to teach his church and us today, that it should not be surprising that the Messiah comes to help those who need help: sinners. The Pharisees expected the Messiah to come for the "right" ones and to set up a kingdom for them, not to aid or help sinners. Levi is the example that Jesus uses even before the controversy at the dinner. Jesus' call is to those who need it, like Levi, those who recognize the call. Therefore, the call is not for the "right" ones because they do not need it and do not recognize the call, especially to repentance. When Jesus comes the second time, will the "right" ones recognize Him, or will He surprise them and call sinners to repentance? Too often we, like the Pharisees, want to mold God to our image rather than being conformed to His image. Our danger is judging or prejudging others. Our danger is holding ourselves aloof from others, not realizing that our own sins—deceit, lack of trust, white lies, pride, arrogance, selfishness, and others—are just as bad as murder, stealing, adultery, and other sins that we consider especially bad, and of which we consider ourselves innocent.

This passage also tells us something of the nature of the church. It is not the palace of the "right" ones but a hospital for those who are sick and seeking health. We are all weak. We all need the Physician. We need to share our hospital with others who are sick and need the Physician. God in Jesus extends forgiveness even to outcasts. This is the grace of God in action. This table fellowship picture reminds us of the final bridal feast at the end of time. It was to Mark's church and is also to us a reminder that the Lord's table is a meal for sinners, not saints, and is open to all who seek the healing of the Physician's hand.

Fastings (2:18-22)

The practice of fasting was common in Judaism. It originally represented mourning, either because of a death or because of sin. The only obligatory fasting for Jews was on the Day of Atonement. However, some Jews practiced fasting twice a week. (See Luke 18:12 and Didache 8:1.) Perhaps the fasting by John's disciples concerned his death.

Note that Jesus does not condemn their fasting but simply teaches that it is not appropriate for His learners. Jesus gives an answer to the question by telling three parables. Jesus uses very common events to teach His truth. The first parable begins as a rhetorical question that implies a negative answer. It is totally inappropriate to fast (mourn) at a wedding. There should be rejoicing and feasting, not fasting and mourning. The allusion to the bridegroom is an allusion to Jesus, whose bride is the church. A new beginning is here.

The reference to the bridegroom is clear. The parables about the unshrunk cloth and the new wineskins are not so clear, at least as they relate to answering the question about fasting. Because that is the case, we should understand these two references in the light of the clear reference to the bridegroom. The commonality appears to center around appropriateness. It is not appropriate to mourn at a wedding; it is not appropriate to put new cloth on old cloth; it is not appropriate to put new wine into old wineskins. Everything has a purpose, including fasting. The purpose of fasting is not fulfilled at a wedding. The purpose of new cloth is not fulfilled by putting it on an old garment; in fact, doing so destroys both the old and the new. The purpose of new wine is not fulfilled by putting it in old wineskins; again, it would destroy both the old and the new.

There is to be nothing alongside Jesus. This applies to traditional Judaism, to followers of John the Baptist, to nationalism, and to whatever they or we might want to add. Jesus is the new element; no syncretism is allowed. Jesus makes the issue larger than fasting. This is not a denial of the fact that Christianity is a continuum of Judaism; but that when the Bridegroom is there, a new beginning is also there, and many parts of the old are no longer appropriate or no longer serve the purpose.

Working on the Sabbath (2:23-28)

A part of the old law is the observance of the Sabbath. In this incident, Jesus is reproached by the Pharisees because His followers have reaped grain on the Sabbath. The question is aimed at Jesus because He is held responsible for what His followers do. Exodus 34:21 states that during the plowing and harvest time, the Jew was to observe the Sabbath and was not to work. The Pharisees defined the extent of work: the followers of Jesus had worked and had therefore broken the Sabbath. The intent of Exodus 34:21 is clear, but Jesus' followers were not farmers and had no intent of clearing a field, earning wages, or doing work for other people. They were simply hungry and ate some of the produce from the field through which they were walking.

Jesus answers the Pharisees' questions concerning breaking the Sabbath in three statements. First, He relates an incident concerning David and his followers where they ate the bread of the Presence, which was only to be eaten by the priests. David broke the law, but he was not condemned by the high priest or by Saul who later found out about the bread. David is nowhere condemned by the Pharisees. Jesus is implying that the Pharisees are inconsistent; otherwise they would also condemn David. The Pharisees' interpretation of the law is simply for their own convenience and is not consistent. Jesus elevates the original intent of the law rather than giving the Pharisaic explanation credence. (Jesus handles the issues of "Corban" and divorce the same way; see Mark 7:9-13 and 10:2-9.)

Jesus' second answer to the Pharisees is that the original intent of the law was to benefit man. The Sabbath was created for man. Man did not come into being for the sake of the Sabbath. Rabbi Simeon ben Menasya, a prominent Jewish teacher, said, "The Sabbath is delivered over for your sake, but you are not delivered over to the Sabbath." The intent of the observance of the Sabbath is for the benefit of man. People are more important than programs, buildings, or even time. All the rules and regulations that God gives are for our benefit. When the rules and regulations are found to work against people, they should be abrogated. Man is the supreme object of God's affection. God loves the world of people, not the Sabbath, not Sunday, not the physical world, and not the temple. God loves the world, not himself; so He benefits the world instead of himself. We also should work to benefit others rather than ourselves. We should love people and use things to benefit people, rather than love things and use people to get more things. Are the rules and regulations we exercise for the benefit of the world or for our own benefit? The church should exist for the benefit of the world, that is, to seek and to save the lost. Rules should benefit people rather than become restrictions of personal freedom.

Jesus' third answer to the Pharisees is that the Son of Man (Jesus) is also Lord of the Sabbath. Jesus' followers can do what the Lord of the Sabbath allows, and so Jesus also allows His followers to pick and eat the grain. The little word *also* here demonstrates that Jesus' authority, which has already been demonstrated in healing, exorcisms, and forgiveness, extends to the law.

CHAPTER THREE

Expansion

Mark 3:1-35

Further Healing on the Sabbath (3:1-6)

Mark moves the plot of his story forward several ways in this account. First, he includes a demonstration of the pronouncement at the end of the last paragraph by showing that Jesus as the Son of Man has authority again to heal, even on the Sabbath. The plot also thickens in this incident because the Pharisees are looking for reasons to trap Jesus. At the conclusion of the event, the Pharisees and the Herodians plot how they can kill Jesus.

Jesus goes into a synagogue on the Sabbath, and a man is there with a dried out hand. (It is probably paralyzed and without being able to be exercised—it is simply skin stretched over bones.) The Pharisees question whether Jesus will heal (work) on the Sabbath. If Jesus works on the Sabbath, then the Pharisees will be able to bring a legal accusation against Him in court for breaking the Mosaic law.

Jesus faces the question directly. He asks the man to stand up and come into the center. This is not a secret healing; rather, Jesus sets up a direct challenge to the Pharisees. Jesus turns from the man for a moment and addresses the Pharisees with the legal question, "Is it legal on the Sabbath to do good or to do bad, to save a life or to kill?" (Mark 3:4, A.T.). Put another way, "Is it legal to heal a person (to do good) or to refrain from healing a person (to do bad)?" The Pharisees, in their interpretation of the law, allowed a farmer to assist an animal who was in trouble on the Sabbath. But the Pharisees, blinded by their opposition, were silent despite what their own interpretation taught. The Pharisees would not agree with Jesus, that it is right to do good and not to do bad. And they could not disagree, that it is right to do evil and not to do good. Therefore, they could only be silent and keep their anger inside. Jesus' rage, however, was clear. As Jesus looked around, He became angry because their hearts were so hardened. There is no translation for this word except "angry," and it is entirely appropriate in this case. Silence is not always golden. The Pharisees' hearts were so hard that they were unable to make a rational answer. The word *hardened* is translated in the Shipibo language as having ears without holes, which is a very accurate description of the Pharisees. Jesus' next words are for the sick man; He tells him to extend his hand. The man does so, and his hand is restored to wholeness.

This particular incident in Mark does not record the crowd's reaction, but it does record how the Pharisees' reacted. They leave immediately and plot with the Herodians to kill Jesus, not because of the healing itself, but because Jesus has overturned their teaching and undermined their authority by His direct challenge. What was true for Jesus' audience is true for Mark's—and for us. The good news about Jesus, His teachings and works, softens many, like the crowds who react with amazement and bring more people to Him. But the good news also hardens some, like the Pharisees and Herodians, who have ears but do not hear, and eyes but do not see.

Another valuable application of this text, which perhaps was not intended by Mark, concerns the use of silence. Silence in the face of evil is not the proper reaction. If we expect good to triumph, we should promote it in every way we can. If we expect evil to be defeated, we must fight it in every way we can. Silence in the face of evil is really the promotion of evil.

The Calling of His Learners (3:7-19)

Probably because of the presence of deadly conflict before the appropriate time (Mark 3:6), Jesus withdraws from the urban area with His learners. However, a large crowd from all around Galilee follows Him to the lake. In fact, many people from the South (Judea and Idumea), the East (beyond Jordan), and the Northwest (Tyre and Sidon) come to Him. They come because they have heard all the things that He did. It becomes evident in Mark 3:9 and 10 that they had heard about Jesus' healing powers and were mainly interested in those powers.

The press of the crowd is so great that Jesus asks the learners to get an escape boat ready. (The crowds were all reaching out to touch Him, believing that touching Him would cure their illnesses.) The Syrophoenician woman in Mark 5:28 had heard about the power of touching Him. The word for diseases here is peculiar because it is normally translated "scourge." It was believed by some that illnesses were scourges from God.

Some people in the crowd were apparently possessed by unclean spirits. The words *unclean spirits, evil spirits,* and *demons* are really synonyms. When these people came into Jesus' presence, the unclean spirits in them fell down and acknowledged that Jesus was the Son of God. Here we have another instance where Jesus orders their silence but only after they have made their confession.

This section of Mark simply gives a summary of the service of Jesus, which is a preview of the next sections of the Gospel. The authority, power, and popularity of Jesus are being taught by Mark to his church. It is curious that although Jesus does not want the testimony of the evil spirits, Mark chooses to include this event in his Gospel as another way of demonstrating the power and authority of Jesus, particularly by his use of the phrase *Son of God.* However, Jesus does not want the testimony of a non-follower. It is not acceptable. The ones who say, "Lord, Lord," but do not follow are not accepted by Jesus either in His service or in His church, either in Mark's time or in ours.

Jesus retreats further from the cities and the crowds that follow Him by going into the hills surrounding the lake. While there, He calls to himself those whom He wants. He calls twelve men whom he also names "apostles" or "delegates." Jesus had two reasons for choosing these twelve men:

[1] "that they might be with him," and
[2] "that he might send [them] off
 [a] to announce [good news], and
 [b] to have authority to drive out demons" (Mark 3:14, 15, A.T.).

It is important to note that the verb *send off* is the same word as the noun *apostle.* A modern synonym would be *delegate;* so the text would read, "That He might delegate the delegates to announce good news." The first purpose of the delegates was to be with Jesus. Remember that in choosing a successor to Judas, the new one had to have been with Jesus from the beginning (Acts 1:21). It is necessary to be with Jesus in order for the delegates to accomplish their second purpose, that is, to announce good news and to throw out demons. These delegates proclaim the good news both during Jesus' service and after His death, burial, and resurrection. The former announcement was, "The kingdom of God is near"; the latter, "The kingdom of God can be entered by trust in the good news that Jesus was crucified for our sins and resurrected on the third day that we might have life eternal." The delegates' service was also to include having authority to throw out demons. The power to throw out demons was a demonstration that the new kingdom was more powerful than the demons and that the new kingdom had indeed arrived in the person of Jesus and in the authority of His delegates.

The term *Twelve* is used absolutely as the name for the group Jesus selected from among those who were following Him. The names of the Twelve are listed with some interesting additions. Simon is named "Peter." James and John are named "Sons of Thunder" or "Sons of Excitement" (cf. Mark 9:38 and Luke 9:54). Another Simon is referred to as "the Canaanean," which in Aramaic means "Zealot," and is so translated in the New International Version. It is a name for the fiery anti-Rome, prone-to-violence group. Mark lists Judas Iscariot at the end with the ominous description that shows early in the story that Judas is the one who ultimately turns Jesus over to the authorities.

This section gives a good picture of the various followers of Jesus. The mass of crowds come because they have heard about Jesus and many want to be healed. Jesus also has learners who have followed more closely. Then Jesus selects the Twelve to be with Him. The role for the Twelve is not significant beyond Jewish Christianity. In fact, God had to specifically call a new delegate, Paul, to go to the Gentiles. The Twelve begins with Simon Peter, the most prominent of the Twelve, and ends with Judas, the most ignominious.

The description of the Twelve, however, reveals an inner circle of three. The inner three (Peter, James, and John) are the first three chosen by Jesus. This is made clear by the fact that Andrew, the brother of Simon Peter, is not listed with Peter, but after the two brothers, James and John. These inner three are indicated further in the section on the transfiguration and in Gethsemane.

The Opposition of Family, Friends, and Scribes (3:20-35)

Mark uses a literary device in Mark 3:20-35 that inserts an event between two phases of another event. The rejection of Jesus by

His family begins in verses 20 and 21, then the rejection of Jesus by the scribes from Jerusalem is told (verses 22-30). The completion of the rejection by Jesus' family finally comes in verses 31-35. This literary device is used six times by Mark. The most obvious place is in Mark 5:21-43, when the healing of the woman with a blood flow interrupts the healing of Jairus's daughter. Mark uses events within events that interpret each other, as we will see in this section.

Jesus returns from the sea and the hills to His home (Mark 3:20). This is certainly a reference to the place where He normally stayed in Capernaum. Mark continues to illustrate Jesus' popularity with the people by saying there was such a great crowd in and around the house that He and His followers could not even eat.

The next sentence literally says, "The ones alongside Him, having heard, went out to seize Him; for they were saying, 'He is standing outside himself'" (Mark 3:21, A.T.). It is certainly not His followers who go out to seize Him, and the great crowds are the ones causing the problems; so to whom is Mark referring as the ones who go out to seize Him? The scribes would like to seize Him, but they would never be described as the "ones alongside Him." Many commentators believe that Mark's expression refers to Jesus' family. The Gospel of John shows that Jesus' brothers did not believe in Him (John 7:3-5). The family was concerned because Jesus' behavior created such great crowds, and according to this verse, He was not able to take care of His own needs. The family sets out to seize Jesus. *Seize* is used later in Mark 6:17 to describe what Herod does when he sends men to "arrest" John the Baptist. Jesus' family apparently thinks that He is insane, that is, literally, "outside himself." They feel that they must seize Him for His own sake and take Him home.

The scribes from Jerusalem are the legal authorities, or lawyers, who have come from the capital to the countryside to investigate this popular person and the wild claims that are made about Him. The fact that Jesus has even drawn the attention of such big-city legal authorities is very unusual. Mark immediately cites the two accusations against Jesus. Note that earlier (in Mark 3:2), some of Jesus' opponents were seeking to make legal accusations against Him. The first accusation is that He is possessed by Beelzebul. *Beelzebul* is probably a reference to Baalzebul, a Canaanite god of the Old Testament with whom Elijah fought on Mt. Carmel. The name means "Baal the Prince."

The second accusation is that He throws out demons in or by the power of the ruler of demons. The phrases *the ruler of demons* and *Baal the Prince* mean the same thing. Note that in Mark 3:30, the opponents say that Jesus has an unclean spirit. Jesus was well known for His throwing out of demons.

Jesus answers the two accusations in two ways. First, He calls the scribes and asks them a rhetorical question. Jesus answers the question with three statements. Note that Jesus equates Beelzebul, the prince of demons, with Satan. The rhetorical question can only be answered in one way: Satan cannot throw out Satan. Just as a kingdom or a house that is divided against itself cannot stand, neither could Satan stand if he were fighting against himself. If he were fighting against himself, it would be a sure sign that he has an end. Second, Jesus tells a brief parable that cannot be denied by the scribes. You have to be stronger than the strong man in order to enter his house and plunder his possessions.

Jesus' answer can be summarized in two sentences. Since Satan cannot throw out Satan and demons are being thrown out by Jesus, then obviously Jesus cannot be Satan or a demon. Since the one throwing out must be stronger than the ones being thrown out, and Jesus throws out demons, then Jesus must be stronger than the demons He throws out.

The throwing out of demons was a demonstration of the power of God. In Luke 11:20 (A.T.), Jesus says, "If I by the finger of God throw out demons, then the kingdom of God has come to you." In Matthew 12:28 the expression *Spirit of God* is used in place of *finger of God,* but the meaning is identical. The coming of the kingdom of God is demonstrated by God's power in overcoming evil. Good overcomes evil. Right is stronger than wrong. The expulsion of demons was a sign of the intrusion of the kingdom and power of God, particularly as it is seen in the mission of Jesus, who throws out the demons. The scribes' accusations against Jesus are an attempt to call the kingdom of God the kingdom of Satan. This is a perversion of the good news. It describes the good as bad. It calls the light darkness. Mark is probably also pointing out to his readers the anomaly that the very ones who should show the way, the legal interpreters of the Mosaic law, are the ones who totally reverse and reject the fulfiller of the Mosaic law.

In the context of this kind of perversion, Mark discusses blasphemy against the Holy Spirit. Blasphemy means to speak against or to insult, especially in reference to God. All other sins can be forgiven, but insulting the Holy Spirit is an eternal sin. The Jews had other unforgivable sins, such as profaning the name of God, because God took His vengeance immediately. Also, anyone who gave false witness in a capital trial was said to be guilty of an unforgivable sin. Mark notes Jesus' seriousness about this matter when he uses the "amen" expression ("I tell you the truth," Mark 3:28) at the beginning of Jesus' statement. The question that arises concerning this passage is why does Jesus single out the Spirit? The Spirit is the power of God. To deny or insult the Spirit is to cut off the power. Remember that Matthew records Jesus' saying, "If I drive out demons by the Spirit of God . . ." (Matthew 12:28). Mark's personal comment (Mark 3:30) also makes this connection because the scribes accused Jesus of having an unclean spirit when the Spirit was, in fact, the Holy Spirit and not an unclean spirit. Inherently, it means that whoever rejects the Holy Spirit as the power in Jesus and in Christianity rejects God, and since all forgiveness comes from God, the sin has eternal consequences.

The text in Mark 3:28-30 does not say that anyone there has committed such blasphemy, but Jesus issues a very stern warning that is applicable to the scribes, to Mark's audience, and to us. Here is the real perversion: the one who comes and throws out Satan by God's Holy Spirit so that men might have life eternal is himself called Satan. Whoever does this has no hope because he is so perverted he says white is black and darkness is light, the work of God is the work of Satan, good is evil and evil is good.

The scribes' rejection is contrasted by the way the crowds accept Jesus. In Mark 3:31-35, Jesus' mother, brothers, and sisters have arrived to take Him home. They ask Him to come outside and go with them. The word is relayed to Jesus that His mother and family are asking for Him. Then Jesus utters an astonishing statement that identifies His real family. The real family of Jesus are the ones who do what God wants. Luke's parallel passage says, "The ones hearing and doing the word of God" (Luke 8:21, A.T.) The fact that the real family of Jesus are the ones who do the will of God or, as I have stated it, the "want" of God, demonstrates that people have a choice. Some around Jesus who have listened to Him have decided to do what God wants. Others, the scribes and Jesus' family, have decided to do what they want. You must do what Jesus wants in order to be a part of His actual family. Jesus' physical family and the interpreters of the law, who ought to have accepted Him, have, in fact, rejected Him. The crowd who gather around Jesus are His true family, the ones who are hearing and doing the Word of God.

This passage, directed to Mark's audience, is a stern warning against rejecting Jesus. It is also an assurance that if we choose to do what God wants, then we will hear and do the Word of God, and we will become a part of the real family of God.

CHAPTER FOUR

Parables and Miracles

Mark 4:1—5:43

Parables: Parallel Story Teaching (4:1-34)

The fourth chapter of Mark, a continuation of chapter 3, concerns the responsibilities of Jesus' followers, His real family. Put another way, it concerns those who hear the Word and do God's will, the insiders. The scene is set in Mark 4:1 and 2, with a large crowd pressing Jesus so much that, in order to teach them at a reasonable distance, He has to sit in a boat that is bobbing in the water. Jesus teaches them by telling parables. These are ordinary stories that have parallel spiritual meanings. But Jesus' use of parables also includes what are called similes and metaphors. This chapter contains all three kinds of parables; so a discussion concerning the audience for whom the parables are intended is important. The parable of the seed is spoken in verses 3-8, and then explained in verses 14-20. In between, Jesus talks about the mystery of the parable and its understanding.

Story of Seed and Soil (1-9, 14-20)

The parable is not really about the sower; otherwise, we could ask why he sowed the seed on the path or on the rocks or among the thorns. The parable is not really about the seed that is sown. The seed is the Word, the Word of the kingdom, or, put another way, the Word of God. In this section in particular, the seed means the teaching of Jesus. The point of the parable concerns human reactions to the message of Jesus. The various reactions center around how one hears. Note that Jesus begins the parable with the command, "Listen!" (Mark 4:3) or "Hear!" and ends the parable with the refrain, "He who has ears to hear, let him hear" (Mark 4:9). Note also that in each of the four cases, every one of them hears, but after hearing, something happens.

Note that what they hear is the Word. The lack of the Word is what causes the difference between the growth on the good soil

45

and no growth on the other soils. Satan takes the Word on the path away. Affliction or persecution on account of the Word causes stumbling in the rocky section. Cares, deceit, and desires choke the Word in the thorny section so that it becomes unfruitful. The Word multiplies only in the good soil, and this is because they not only hear the Word but welcome it. The opposition to the Word does not come solely from Satan. The Word is heard and responded to in the rocky section, but when affliction or persecution comes along, people are offended and leave the Word behind. The cares (concerns, anxieties, or worries) of the age, the deceitfulness of wealth, and the desires for things that come into the life of those who hear the Word cause problems in the thorny area. All these cares and desires choke out the Word with the result that this person's life becomes unfruitful.

The purpose of any seed is to produce fruit. Some seed fails to produce fruit because of the nature of the person's life into which the seed is sown. That person hears the Word but is not willing to do the Word. Remember that Jesus' real family is composed not of the ones hearing, but of the ones doing, the will of God. Jesus is telling His audience, and Mark is telling his church and us that listening to the Word is simply not sufficient. The Word, which is the teaching of Jesus, must be heard, welcomed, and allowed to grow.

The type of sowing that is illustrated in this parable is broadcast sowing, or scattering the seed. Contrary to the parable where the path is clear, we do not know in advance the reaction of people to whom the good news is proclaimed. But we should be neither fatalistic (assuming everyone to be the path-type soil) nor should we expect 100% reception. Where we can, we should prepare the ground. Those people who heard once can hear again, but once they reject the Word, it is easier for them to reject it again. We should prepare the ground carefully and sow the seed as carefully as we can.

The Word is interpreted as the teachings of Jesus. We hear or read His teachings frequently. It is not a matter of our hearing the teachings but of our doing something that is critical. We know that fruit is produced by such activities as planting, watering, fertilizing, and pruning. As James, Jesus' brother, said, "Be ... doers of the word and not hearers only" (James 1:22, KJV)

The point of the parable is that we should hear the Word of God and then translate that hearing into action.

The Understanding of Stories (10-13, 33, 34)

These two paragraphs give some understanding about how the parables were viewed by Jesus' audience. The first section is Jesus' own words about the parables, and the second section is Mark's understanding of Jesus' use of parables. Mark 4:10 indicates that more than Jesus' chosen Twelve were there when He was asked about the meaning of parables. The ones around Him remind us of the ones around Jesus when His mother and brothers came searching for Him. Note that they are also asking about parables (plural), not simply the parable Mark has just narrated. Jesus replies to the ones around Him that they have been given the mystery of the kingdom of God. *Mystery* (a transliteration of the word in the text) is a better word to use here than *secret*. The word *mystery* is used in the epistles, but it is a mystery that God wants made known, that is, that the Gentiles are to be accepted. In the mystery religions that surrounded early Christianity, mysteries were the secret words or phrases that indicated initiation into the religion. These were thought to be powerful words that made the deity work for the person. This is the only occurrence of the word *mystery* in the Gospels. As in the epistles, it is made known—but only to the ones who hear and do. The mystery is only mysterious to the unwilling. As John 7:17 says, "If one wills to do His will, he will know . . ." (A.T.)

The ones "outside" are the ones who have heard but do not understand or do. The expression *outside* occurs twice at the end of chapter 3 to describe the physical family of Jesus instead of describing those who are gathered inside listening to Jesus. The reference to parables here is not simply to the parallel stories that Jesus tells, but probably means riddles or secrets, which is a broader meaning than we normally have.

When Jesus quotes from Isaiah 6:9 (in Mark 4:12), He is showing what the parable of the sower showed: that only the ones doing really understand. Isaiah 6 contains the call of God to Isaiah to speak for God. In the process, God told Isaiah how stubborn Judah would be. Judah would see but not perceive, they would hear but not understand; because if they really saw and heard, they would turn and be forgiven. This is a picture of God's experience with Israel throughout its history. God brings the Israelites out of Egypt, but they complain in the desert about lack of food. God gives them a land flowing with milk and honey; yet they worship other gods who have not given them provisions.

Again and again, God sends prophets to tell them the Word of God.

Israel hears and sometimes understands, but more often ignores the Word. Isaiah can expect that kind of reception. The Christian evangelist can also expect a similar reception. This is also the message of the parable of the sower. What is meant to give light (a parable) becomes a mystery. People can hear the parables, but only the ones hearing and welcoming the Word will understand and then produce fruit. This is like the proclamation of the good news. People can hear it, too, but it is good news only to those who hear and accept. It becomes bad news to those who hear the same words but reject them.

All of us can hear the parables, but we must not be like Israel and be hard of hearing and understanding. We must hear and then do.

Jesus knows that His followers do not completely understand the parables; so He follows the story with an explanation. Mark explains (Mark 4:33, 34) that Jesus spoke the word to them (the crowds) in many parables, but only to the extent that they were able to understand. But privately, Jesus explained the parables in more detail to His learners. Even Jesus' closest learners did not always clearly understand His explanations. For example, Jesus will later talk about His approaching death and resurrection three times. The learners will hear Jesus speak, but they will not comprehend what He says. In fact, Peter at one point will even begin to rebuke Jesus.

Mark's audience has the advantage of knowing the end of the story; so many of the parables are clear to them. But they are believers, and parables are clear to those who have heard and obeyed. The Word of the kingdom is also clear to us. We have not only the parables, but also Jesus' explanations. But Christianity is still a mystery to those who are "outside." Many hear the words but do not comprehend their meaning. Many see concepts but do not perceive their conclusions. Our task is to continue to proclaim the good news, to sow the seed of the Word, so that some might fall on good ground and produce fruit.

Be Careful Listeners (21-25)

Mark has put two proverbial sayings (Mark 4:21, 25) with explanations for each in this section. Between the two is the encouraging refrain, "If anyone has ears to ear, let him hear" (Mark

4:23). This entire section is also about hearing, just as the parable of the sower was about hearing.

The text actually says that the "lamp comes." Certainly this is a reference to Jesus as the lamp or the light. Jesus' coming and His teaching are to be seen, not to be hidden. They are to be welcomed, not rejected. The only proper place for a lamp is on a lampstand, and the only proper place for the light of the world is where it can be seen. Jesus may have been in partial obscurity during His service, but through His cross experience, Jesus' real nature and mission have come to light. We should be even more careful to listen to His words because this is true. This is the encouragement of Mark 4:23. Remember again that hearing the Word is not sufficient; we must also do what the Word says.

Mark 4:24 begins with the encouragement to be very careful how you hear, because the more you hear and do, the more you will be able to receive and continue to hear and do. If you have begun the process of hearing and doing, then you will receive more. If you do not hear, then you will lose even what you may have had.

This section calls us to hear responsibly. If we allow the Word to go "in one ear and out the other," we have not understood the purpose of a lamp, nor have we been careful how we listen.

The Seed Stories (26-32)

Both of the seed parables concern the kingdom of God. The kingdom is not a place (like the United Kingdom) or a specific time period, but an age when individuals accept the reign of God for their lives. The kingdom comes when one accepts God's authority in his life. The kingdom comes ultimately and completely when God asserts His full authority at the end of time over all beings. But the kingdom is also here now when individuals and churches accept the reign or sovereignty of God.

Both parables also have the commonality of a seed. This is similar to the seed in the first parable in the chapter. The seed is still the Word of God or the teachings of Jesus as He teaches the Word of God. These two parables then reflect on what happens to the seed.

The first parable concentrates on the agricultural cycle. Normally, a parable is a whole with one point. The parable of the sower is an exception. This parable of the automatically growing seed really has one point. We should not try to identify the meaning of the man, seed, ground, blade, grain, and harvest separately. The point is that the kingdom is like the whole process of sowing seed, the seed's growing, and the fruit of the seed's being harvested at the end of the cycle. The kingdom, once sown, will grow "automatically." *Automatically* is a transliteration of the Greek word for "by itself." The parable reflects both the certainty of growth and the certainty of harvest. When and how these occur are in God's hands, but the certainty is there by promise. The Word of God, spread by the people who accept the reign of God, will grow and produce more people who accept the reign of God in their lives. The seed will do this automatically because it is God's Word.

The mustard seed mentioned here is the Word of God as it is in the other parables. It's growth is also a natural consequence. But the real point to this parable is that though the seed has small beginnings, its ultimate end will be much larger than its size indicates. The conclusion is perhaps meant to indicate the inclusion of non-Jews in the kingdom. If so, the book of Acts is a portrayal of this parable. The word begins in Jerusalem in A.D. 30 with 120 believers. The book of Acts ends in Rome, the center of the civilized world, in A.D. 64, with thousands of believers. The Word had a small beginning, but even then the potential for phenomenal growth was there. This parable is sure to bring assurance to Mark's church that although they may seem small in comparison to the rest of the world, they are on the right side, and they will have a very large impact.

Perhaps there is also a call in these two parables to be faithful to the seed. The middle parables call us to hear the Word of God carefully, and not simply to hear, but to do.

Miracles (4:35—5:43)

A Nature Miracle (4:35-41)

Following this series of parables, Jesus again crosses the sea with His followers. A great windstorm stirs up large waves, which start to swamp the boat. The boat is in real danger; it is filling with water. The followers, some of whom are fishermen, know this lake well, and they are afraid that they might drown. Meanwhile, Jesus is sleeping soundly on a pillow in the stern. He is unaware of the windstorm, the violent rocking waves, or the water that is rapidly filling the boat. This picture of Jesus brings to mind the Psalms that say, "I lie down and sleep; I wake again, because the Lord sustains me" (Psalm 3:5), and, "I will lie down and sleep in peace, for you alone, O Lord, make me dwell in safety" (Psalm 4:8). Jesus was wholly dependent on God. He demonstrated His trust by being able to sleep soundly even during a violent storm.

The small details in this account have the marks of incidental accuracy and eyewitness material. Jesus is in the stern and His head is on a pillow. These details are not essential to the story; so there is no reason for them to be there, except the storyteller was at the event and gives the details he saw. Papias, an early church father, relates that Mark wrote down Peter's remembrances of the incident.

In the face of real danger, the men decide to waken Jesus to see whether He will rescue them. They simply do not know what else to do. While we do not have the full conversation, we do have a series of questions, two asked by the men and two asked by Jesus. When Jesus is awake, the men ask Him, "Do you not care that we are being destroyed?" (Mark 4:38, A.T.). While they are afraid of dying, their question to Jesus is about His concern for them. Jesus first controls the windstorm before He deals with the storm of emotions inside His followers. Jesus rebukes the wind and then gives two commands to the sea. "Be quiet! Be muzzled!" (Mark 4:39, A.T.) The wind ceases to blow, and a great calm settles on the sea.

Jesus then asks two questions concerning the men's cowardice and their lack of trust. These questions are strong forms of rebuke. This is the first of several occasions in Mark where the followers are severely rebuked for their lack of trust. Jesus has a concern first for their cowardice. The verb form of cowardice is used in 2 Timothy 1:7 as a negative and the opposite of power, love, and self-control. It is used in Revelation 21:8 in a list along with murderers, adulterers, and faithless, whose ultimate end is the lake of fire or second death. The followers are cowards; they depend on Jesus without struggling and taking responsibilities for themselves or depending on God as Jesus does (remember He continued to sleep during the storm).

The second question Jesus asks is literally, "How have you not trust?" (Mark 4:40, A.T.). Another reading can be translated, "Do you not yet have trust?" The book of Luke, in the parallel passage, has the question, "Where is your trust?" (Luke 8:25,

A.T.) No matter how it is translated, Jesus is concerned about their lack of trust. These men have been with Him for some time; they have seen Him heal and perform other miracles; so where is their trust? By this time, they should have some trust in His power. Perhaps their trust is only in Jesus when He is awake. How should trusting men have acted in this situation? Was the choice they had between cowardice and trust?

The final question in this story is asked by the learners, and they ask themselves and not Jesus. "Who then is this one, that even the wind and the sea obey Him?" (Mark 4:41, A.T.) Everyone knows that both the winds and the sea are not controlled by men; yet Jesus speaks to them and controls them. Psalm 107:25-30 speaks about God's power over the sea. The learners' concern is that they do not really know who Jesus is. Is He God? How can He be? They are always surprised by His power.

Mark relates this story to his church to build their trust in Jesus. They must trust in the One who commands the wind and sea. Mark's church is in the middle of great persecution. Even as the boat is guided safely through the storm, the struggling church will be led safely through persecution. Jesus is there to restore calm and trust in the face of fear and death. Our lesson to learn is to trust.

The end of this narrative has a question that is asked by the learners, but is not answered. Mark tends to leave a number of events with unanswered questions. I believe he intends that his reading/listening audience should answer the questions for themselves. Who is Jesus? Will you trust Him? We ask these questions as we read Mark's text. Mark's audience and people today should have the same immediate answer. Jesus is the Christ, the Son of the living God.

We also experience rough seas, and sometimes we act just like Jesus' followers. Family hostilities, accidents, divorce, children's problems, severe illnesses, and deaths occur, and our first reaction is often, "Where is God? Why me? Don't You care about me, God?" Sometimes we fear for our lives or our sanity. Why do we have rough seas, these problems? Why can't we be calm and serene Christians? When problems appear, the first thing we want is a miracle. Is our trust in calm seas or Jesus? Do we trust Him unconditionally or only when He is awake? Even though we grow through unexpected events in our life, we would rather avoid them. How can we demonstrate our trust in God in disruptive times? Who is this Person whom even the winds and the sea obey? He is the Christ, the Son of the living God.

Healing a Man Possessed by Many Demons (5:1-20)

Mark continues his theme concerning Jesus' authority into chapter 5, but now his theme is expanded to include a discussion of unclean things. He gives us three instances: (1) there is an unclean spirit in a man who lives among tombs (an unclean place) in an area outside of Israel (also unclean), and the unclean spirits enter into pigs (unclean animals), (2) Jesus raises a dead girl (the dead are unclean), and (3) a woman with a hemorrhage (unclean) touches Jesus. Mark's narrative shows us that Jesus' power and authority extends to clean the unclean, whether they are Jewish or not.

The setting for the first section (Mark 5:1-20) is the southeast edge of the sea of Galilee near the Decapolis, which is a loose association of ten cities. The exact place is not known, although Gerasa is the most likely place.

After Jesus calms the storm, His boat puts into shore, and a man with an unclean spirit approaches. Mark gives a detailed description of the man's circumstances. He lived among the tombs, probably caves in the area where the local people buried their dead. Because the man was wild, he had been shackled several times. He had succeeded in breaking his chains, and at this time ran unsubdued. His actions were insane: he shouted, ran naked, and cut himself with rocks.

This wild man sees Jesus from a distance, runs and falls down in front of Him, and acknowledges Him. The demon speaks through the man and addresses Jesus as "the Son of the Most High God" (Mark 5:7). This title is an Old Testament expression used mostly by non-Israelites.

The demon has two concerns. First, he wants to know what Jesus has to do with him. Second, he wants Jesus to swear an oath that Jesus will not torment him. Jesus commands the demon to leave the man. Jesus does this without being asked by the man.

The conversation with the demon concerning his name reveals that he is not just one, but many demons. Jesus asks the demons' names because this is a way of having power over demons. The name *Legion* is a Latin word that often refers to the armies of the Emperor. A Roman legion in Emperor Augustus' day had approximately 6,000 men. The actual count of demons in the man is given as 2,000 when they enter the pigs (assuming one demon entered each pig).

Mark goes on to describe the conversation between the demons and Jesus. The demons leave the man's body and invade the pigs that are foraging on a nearby hill. The pigs, full of demons, rush down the hill and drown in the lake. The demons get their wish not to have to leave the area, but they are still destroyed when the pigs rush headlong to their destruction.

Perhaps Mark tells most of the narrative so that he can show two very opposite reactions to the power and authority of Jesus. After the pig herders relate their story in the cities and surrounding countryside, people come out to see for themselves what actually happened. Their first sight is of the man whom they have known to be crazy, naked, and wild. But, to their surprise, the man is sitting, fully clothed, and lucid. People who see this man's abrupt change become uneasy about Jesus and ask Him to leave.

Why were these people so uneasy and afraid? Did they think Jesus might heal other people? Or did they think they might lose more of their possessions (like their pigs)? We cannot be sure why, but they reacted to Jesus' power with fear, a fear that moved them to ask Jesus to leave. As Jesus prepares to leave, the healed man wants to go with Him. The man who has experienced the power of Jesus does not want to leave Jesus' side. But Jesus tells him to go home to his friends and tell them what the Lord has done for him and how the Lord had mercy on him. The man obeys and begins to announce widely what Jesus has done for him. Persons who hear this man are amazed.

We can be amazed at the power of Jesus from a distance, but if He were near, would we be as comfortable? (Reading about miracles is one thing, but seeing one at close range would be unsettling.) The demons know who Jesus is and do not want to be around Him. The city and country people acknowledge what great power Jesus has, but they do not want Him to stay. The healed man feels the power of Jesus and wants to stay near Him, but instead is given the assignment to proclaim God's good news. All the characters in this narrative are aware of the power of God, but awareness paralyzes most of them and energizes only the healed man. Belief in God still has the power to paralyze and energize. Mark wants to energize his audience by relating this demonstration of Jesus' power. He wants his audience to tell others the good news of Jesus. The challenge is there for us also. We can be paralyzed by our faith or we can be energized.

Two Daughters of Israel Are Healed (21-43)

The healing of the synagogue ruler's daughter is interrupted by the story of the healing of the woman with a hemorrhage. This technique in storytelling occurs several times in the book of Mark. In this particular incident, the interruption is not only a literary technique, but probably a historical recollection, since the other Gospels have the same sequence. The interruption in the narrative builds suspense because at the beginning of the story, the daughter of the synagogue ruler is close to death; an interruption may make Jesus too late to do anything. The interruption, however, makes the miracle even greater because instead of a healing, it becomes a resurrection from the dead.

The two incidents are also very similar in several respects. Jesus calls the bleeding woman "daughter" (Mark 5:34), and the synagogue ruler's small daughter is close to death (Mark 5:23). Both are not only healed from disease, but also saved. The Greek word carries both meanings and is peculiarly appropriate. Both are female and both are ritually unclean. One is twelve years old, and the other has had her chronic disease for twelve years.

A progression of Jesus' power and authority is evident in Mark: first, Jesus calms the sea; then He throws out demons; He heals a woman who has never been helped by physicians; and finally, He brings a young girl back to life.

The setting for this action begins alongside the sea of Galilee when Jesus returns from the country of the Gerasenes. A crowd gathers to hear Him, which is a sharp contrast from the earlier crowd that had invited Him to leave because they did not want to hear Him. Jairus comes to Jesus. Forgetting his position as a ruler of the synagogue, he falls at Jesus' feet. References in the New Testament indicate that synagogue rulers are charged with the order of the services, maintenance of the buildings, and protection of the synagogue's integrity (Luke 13:14; Acts 13:15). The ruler asks Jesus to come see his daughter and lay His hands on her so that she might be healed and live. The ruler had obviously heard about Jesus earlier and already believed that Jesus could heal. The others doubt whether Jesus would go home with the ruler, but Jesus overcomes that doubt and does as He is asked.

The crowd follows Jesus. A woman who had a hemorrhage for twelve years also has heard what Jesus is able to do, and also follows Jesus. She does not have the courage or position to ask Jesus for help as the ruler does. She wants healing, not publicity. But she also believes, and she believes that if she can just touch His clothes that she will be healed. The woman is in a desperate situation. She has tried all the physicians and, in fact, has spent all her resources trying to find a cure (Mark 5:26). In spite of her efforts, her condition is worse. She is ritually unclean because of her flow of blood (Leviticus 15:25-27), and she should never have approached Jesus directly.

Many had touched Jesus in the movement of such a crowd of people, but this woman purposefully reaches to touch Jesus in full trust. She has no doubt and is healed immediately. Jesus knows the healing has happened because He feels power leave Him. This is a unique expression in the New Testament and difficult to understand. Jesus knew something had happened, but how and to whom? Jesus looks for the particular person who touched Him. The learners do not understand His motivation since the crowd includes so many people. The woman comes forward, even though she is trembling with fear.

Why does she come to Jesus now when earlier she did not feel she could? She has been healed and comes to Jesus filled with awe because of what has happened to her through the power of this Man. Her fear and trembling is not a negative reaction, but a very appropriate one when approaching such power and authority. She, just as the synagogue ruler did before her, falls at Jesus' feet to demonstrate her respect, awe, and thankfulness. She tells Him her story. Jesus' loving address to her is, "Daughter, your trust has saved you" (Mark 5:34, A.T.). The Hebrew greeting of *shalom* or *peace* is a consequence of salvation. Included with salvation is her new health: Jesus has healed her of her disease and has given her an assurance of wholeness. The woman has been healed—made whole—and she receives peace.

The story of the small daughter continues when word is received that she is dead. The messengers tell their ruler not to bother or annoy the Teacher further. Jesus ignores the message and tells the ruler, "Do not continue to fear, but continue trusting" (Mark 5:36, A.T.).

Arriving at the ruler's home, Jesus invites His inner three to be with Him. The professional mourners are already at work: they are weeping, wailing, and making a great uproar. The child is truly dead. But Jesus denies the finality of that death and asserts that the child is not dead but is only asleep. The mourners respond with mocking laughter. The expression *sleep* is often used in the New Testament as a euphemism for death, but Jesus denies death here, perhaps to avoid the publicity that a resurrection would bring. Note also that He warns them later not to tell about the child's revival. The mourners are ejected from the house and Jesus enters the child's room. He holds the little girl's hand and speaks to her (in Aramaic), telling her to get up.

Mark uses more Aramaic words than all the other Gospels. This is an indication of his Gospel's closeness to Aramaic-Palestinian sources and is another indication of eyewitness sources. Mark's audience, however, needs a translation, and Mark helpfully provides it.

The general reaction to Jesus' miracles is amazement. Despite the trust of the father and the following of the inner three, the immediate reaction is amazement, not confidence. How could such an exciting event be kept secret, as Jesus seems to desire? Mark's audience would ask themselves such a question, and their answer would be, "We must tell other people." Jesus, however, wants to avoid publicity. His time has not yet come. After His own resurrection, there will be no necessity for secrets, but for the current time, Jesus wants as little publicity as possible. Mark's eyewitness account is further demonstrated by the small detail of Jesus' concern for the little girl's hunger. The fact that she is able to eat is also a confirmation to everyone that she is not simply a ghost, but is alive.

The major point in both these healings concerns trust. The woman's trust led her to touch Jesus, and she was healed. The ruler's trust led him to ask Jesus to come home with him. Jesus encouraged the ruler's trust even in the face of death. The trust of each person is strengthened when the healings occur. The trust is in the power and authority of Jesus. Trust is still valid for Mark's church, although Jesus is not with them physically. Jesus has been resurrected and is still alive. His power and authority are still real; therefore, trust is still the way to approach Him.

The person who exercises power over an incurable disease that physicians cannot cure and the person who exercises power over death has himself overcome death. Therefore, He can still exercise His power for Christians today. Persecution in Mark's church was real. Death was a possibility because of persecution. Like the father who still feared, we still fear death, but that should not mean that we should face death without hope. Death was not final for the little girl. Death is not final for the Christian. Do not continue to fear. Continue to trust. These are exhortations to the ruler then and to us today. Christ will make you alive. Fear and trust are not opposites. In the real world, we must live with fear, but we should also choose to live with trust. The stronger our trust is, the less fear we will have.

Sometimes we expect that since Jesus healed people in His own day that He should continue to do so now, and in the same miraculous ways. The actions of Jesus include no set formula for healing. Note that the demoniac did not ask to be healed, but Jesus healed him anyway. The woman did not even ask, but trusted in her actions and Jesus' power, and He healed her. The little girl was not conscious, but she was healed because her father trusted Jesus.

God is alive today and active in many ways. People are healed today by surgery, by medicine, by their body's own defense mechanisms, and sometimes through ways that we do not totally understand. There is not just one way for healing to occur, and no magical formula that Jesus uses to heal us.

CHAPTER FIVE

Popularity

Mark 6:1-56

Rejection (6:1-6)

Jesus' rejection in Nazareth follows right after His acceptance at the Sea of Galilee, which in turn follows His rejection by the Gadarenes. This is an important sequence for Jesus' learners because Jesus is about to send them out to preach and heal, and the learners will also meet both acceptance and rejection. The ultimate rejection is death, and Mark reminds his audience that John the Baptist met that fate. The lengthy flashback description is a reminder to the audience that Jesus also died because of persecution.

Jesus returns to His hometown, and His learners follow Him. Jesus' reputation obviously has preceded Him because He is asked to teach on the Sabbath. The people are astonished when He concludes. The contrast between the Jesus they know and the Jesus who has just taught them is enormous. The hometown people had known Jesus from the time He was about two years old until He had left the village to begin His service when He was about thirty years old. He was a carpenter, having learned the trade from His father Joseph. The hometown people knew Jesus' brothers and sisters, all of whom seemed ordinary enough. They also knew Jesus was the son of Mary. "The son of Mary" is an unusual description in Jewish thought, and perhaps indicates the idea that the people thought that Jesus was illegitimate. Even if Joseph were dead, Jesus would normally have been referred to as the son of Joseph. Contrary to many apocryphal stories about Jesus' childhood, apparently Jesus was regarded as having had a normal childhood and young adult life, at least until He returned home this time and taught in the local synagogue.

The local people ask Jesus three questions after His speech in the synagogue. Where did He get His ideas? Certainly not from His local upbringing! What is the wisdom given to Him? This question is an acknowledgment that Jesus has the ability to teach Jewish religious truth from God. And from other parts of Mark, we know that Jesus taught with authority and clarity. These two questions imply that the people recognize the wisdom and authority of what Jesus says. The third question concerns the powerful works He does. This question probably was not asked as a consequence of firsthand information. Mark remarks at the end of the passage that Jesus performed few powerful deeds in the village. The third question is asked because Jesus' reputation for powerful works has spread to His hometown.

Although the questions imply that people recognize His authority and power, the contrast between the local boy and the great teacher is too wide. The people reject Jesus because they are offended at Him. Jesus quotes a proverb common both to Jewish and Greek culture that a hometown boy (prophet, in this case) is generally without honor in his own country, even among his own relatives and in his own house. Mark related earlier that Jesus' family had gone out to seize Jesus and take Him home because they thought He was out of His mind. Everyone there rejects Jesus, including His own family. The astonishment at His teaching leads them to unbelief. This lack of trust means that Jesus is unable to do powerful deeds in His hometown. Rejection automatically results in a lack of trust. If there is no trust, there is no power. Power is the natural result of having trust.

This is a negative example for Mark's church. The church must live by trust if it is going to be powerful. Having little trust means having little power. Since we believe in God and His power, we must demonstrate that by trust. If there is no demonstration of trust, then we cannot expect that God is able to work as powerfully as He would like. As this passage ends, Jesus is marveling at His audience's lack of trust. Normally, it is the crowds that marvel, but Jesus appears genuinely surprised and disappointed that His own hometown will not accept Him.

We think that if we had been in the crowd at Nazareth, we would not have been so hardheaded. Yet time and again, we also reject current information based upon our past experience. Jesus' common, ordinary early life led His villagers to reject the power and authority He later so ably demonstrated.

The possibility of rejection is a theme that Mark wants his audience to understand. Rejection occurs because something may be too familiar or common. Naaman initially rejected bathing in the Jordan river because he felt his doing so was too common (2 Kings 5:10-12). Sometimes, rejection occurs because of jealousy, a real possibility for people who feel comfortable only in their own surroundings, or those who might never have had the opportunity to travel and have new experiences. Rejection occurs because, despite new information, people are frightened of power and wisdom. We often reject the very thing that can help us. For example, the neurotic and the psychotic do things that deliberately cut themselves off from the help they desperately need.

We must see rejection also from the other side. Jesus was surprised at their rejection. Jesus wants His learners to know that rejection is a possibility. Mark also wants his church to know that rejection is a possibility. We, too, need to realize that rejection is a possibility. But rejection did not stop Jesus, He continued to go about the villages teaching. Rejection should not stop us. This passage then leads into the sending out of the Twelve.

Delegation to Mission (6:7-29)

Two by Two Sent Out (7-13)

Jesus has had the learners follow Him in all of His teaching, preaching, and healing. He has modeled for them what He now wants them to do. He summons the Twelve and sends them out two by two. Jesus gives them authority over unclean spirits, which is meant to be a demonstration of the coming power of the kingdom of God, but He also tells them that they are to take no provisions with them, except a staff.

The learners are to depend totally upon the villagers they go to for their support. Specifically, they are not to take bread, nor copper coins, nor two shirts. The prohibited bag that is mentioned probably refers to a beggar's bag that itinerant wise men used to collect funds for support.

Why are they sent with no provisions? Certainly urgency plays a part, but Jesus teaches that the laborer is worthy of his hire and that it is wrong to muzzle the ox who is treading out the grain. Later, Paul taught that those who preach the gospel should live by the gospel (1 Corinthians 9:14).

The learners are to go to one house in a village and remain there during their stay. They are not to go from house to house. They are not to accept a better offer if one should come along. They are to be dependent upon their hearers for their support.

If they are rejected, they are to shake the dust from their sandals as a witness against that village. This is an ancient Hebrew custom. Coming back to Israel from a foreign country, Jews would shake off the dust from the pagan country before entering Israel. A similar practice is referred to in Acts 18:6, where Paul "shook out his clothes." The point of both actions is clear; those who reject must now assume responsibility for themselves.

Verses 12 and 13 seem like a summary of the learner's mission, but verse 30 also appears to be a summary. This is probably another example of Mark's beginning a story, then interrupting it with an incident that helps to explain the story, and then concluding the original story. In this case, the intervening story about John the Baptist's execution serves to show the reader that although the learners will meet with success on their mission, there is also the possibility of persecution.

According to the summary in verses 12 and 13, the learners announced that men should repent, they threw out many demons, and they anointed many ailing people with oil and healed them. The announcement of the need for repentance only made sense if they also announced the coming of the kingdom of God for which people must prepare by changing their minds and actions. Throwing out the demons was accomplished by the authority Jesus had given them. This was a demonstration of the power of God, which was able to defeat the power of the kingdom of the devil and his demons. And just as Jesus healed many, the learners were also able to heal, although they used a common medicinal practice, anointing persons with oil. The healings were a demonstration of God's power working in the learners of Jesus and also of God's love and concern for His people.

Mark wants his readers to develop their trust in the power and authority of Jesus. Mark uses the story of the sending of the Twelve as a model of what learners of Jesus should be doing to continue to spread His kingdom, but it is not an absolute model for imitation. The readers of Mark are aware that the kingdom has in fact come in the death, burial, and resurrection of Jesus. Mark's readers know that all people should repent because Jesus has accomplished salvation through the cross, and only through trust in His name will they be forgiven and delivered.

The necessity for the announcement is the same. The urgency is likewise the same. Perhaps the simplicity of the baggage ought to be the same, also. And, of course, Mark's readers must be aware that some will accept and some will reject. There is danger also for a person on a mission. John the Baptist lost his head, Jesus was crucified, persecution followed the original learners, and Mark's readers also face persecutions.

We are also learners of Christ. We also have been sent with a message. It is still necessary to go, and it is still urgent. There will still be some who accept and some who reject. Perhaps we also need to follow the principle of simplicity so that excess baggage does not deter us from our mission.

Our mission does not literally include throwing out demons or anointing the sick with oil in order to heal them. But the learner of Jesus still must demonstrate both the power and the love of God. That demonstration will vary from mission to mission. It may include concerns about health, hunger, education, or freedom. But it must always include an announcement of the necessity to change from anti-God to God, from sin to rightness, from evil to good. Only when a person has been forgiven can he or she then announce that forgiveness to others.

The importance of the announcement needs to be emphasized. The learners were told in advance to expect rejection. They met both acceptance and rejection just as Jesus had in His service. Our obligation is to make the announcement. If rejection follows, it is not a reflection on our announcement or upon us. We need to shake off the dust—figuratively speaking—and go on to another town or person to make the announcement again. However, if acceptance follows our announcement, we must be careful to acknowledge that the announcement and the power are from God, not from us.

Unfortunate Results of Faithfulness to Mission (14-29)

King Herod hears about Jesus' powerful works as a result of Jesus' continued teaching and healing. This ruler is Herod Antipas, a son of Herod the Great. At his father's death, Herod Antipas received one-fourth of his father's kingdom to rule. King Herod's title, Tetrarch, literally means ruler of one-fourth, and his kingdom consisted of Galilee and Perea. Herod was not technically a king, although he had great aspirations for the designation. It is not surprising to learn that Herod has heard about Jesus. Mark has made very clear that Jesus was extremely popular. (Refer to Mark 1:28, 45; 2:2; 3:8, 20; 4:1.) Here Mark indicates that reports about Jesus had reached even to the politically sensitive ears of Herod Antipas.

Mark gives us an interim evaluation concerning Jesus at this point. Some people think that Jesus is John the Baptist, others think that He is Elijah or another prophet. Jesus' audience, and perhaps also those in Mark's church, seem to have confused John, Jesus, and Elijah in their minds. Mark makes clear that while John is, in effect, a latter-day Elijah (Mark 9:10-13), Jesus is distinguished from Elijah because Elijah must come first. John the Baptist is the Elijah who is also predicted by Malachi as a prophet. Jesus is neither Elijah nor that prophet. Jesus is also not John the Baptist, although as the Son of Man, He will undergo suffering like John. Jesus does not begin His service until after John's imprisonment (Mark 1:14). Jesus is not the prophet, but He will suffer like the prophets and will be dishonored in His own country as they were.

Herod Antipas, however, presumes Jesus is John the Baptist who has been resurrected. Herod hears about His miraculous powers, which the ruler assumes come from John's resurrection. Herod is greatly concerned because he is the one who had John executed! Mark uses this fact to set up a flashback to the time when Herod had John killed.

Mark probably intends that the flashback should remind his church that the successful Twelve also have suffering ahead of them as a natural consequence of their service for God. Mark's audience also knows that suffering is also ahead for Jesus.

Physical suffering was a real part of the lives of Jesus' followers in Biblical times and through several centuries that followed. Physical persecution of Jesus' followers is rare in the western world today, but in non-Christian countries, the possibility of persecution can still be an unfortunate part of a Christian's service.

We have brief descriptions of the main characters in the flashback. Although John the Baptist is the central character in the story, he is not the one in action. John previously had spoken out against Herod's marriage to his brother's wife. The action against John in Mark's account concerns John's earlier remarks. The action is turned toward John, not initiated by him.

Herod Antipas is the main character. He is a very weak man despite his political power. Herod had chosen his first wife merely to seal a political alliance with a neighboring country. He quickly set aside this marriage in order to marry Herodias. Herod seized John the Baptist because Herodias was upset at John's condemnation of their marriage. His wife wanted John executed as punishment, but Herod could not order the deed done. Instead, Herod kept John safe in prison at Macherus near the northeast corner of the Dead Sea. Herod regarded John as a holy and just man and gladly listened to him, but at the same time, John perplexed him, and Herod would not release him. Finally, through a rash oath, Herod puts himself into the dilemma of either breaking his word in front of all his chief supporters or executing John, and he chooses (with politics in mind) the latter.

Herodias was the wife of Herod Antipas's brother, Herod Philip. Their marriage resulted in a daughter, Salome. Herodias acts with Herod much like Jezebel did with Ahab; she wants John killed. It is highly unusual for a princess like Salome to dance before guests at a feast, especially her stepfather's, and especially in such a sensuous way so as to please everyone there, including Herod. We know that Herodias had her daughter ask for John's head; we can presume that Herodias also asked her daughter to dance in order to please Herod.

Salome was a young girl of marriageable age. It is difficult to imagine that she hesitated to fulfill her mother's requests. Salome obviously was a skilled dancer, but she also had a taste for the bizarre. Herodias simply wanted John killed, but it was Salome who thought it would be a nice touch to have John's severed head presented to Herod on a serving platter because a feast was in process.

Mark puts this story in this location in his book to remind his readers that persecution may result from carrying out their mission. We should recall that John the Baptist lived his life before he had any assurance of resurrection, since Jesus had not yet died and been resurrected. Mark's audience, and we, are in a different position. The promise of life after death is a central part of our trust in Jesus.

Nature Miracles (6:30-56)

Feeding of Five Thousand (30-44)

As this section begins, the Twelve are returning to Jesus to relate to Him how they carried out their mission. Mark describes the Twelve as "apostles" (Mark 6:30), probably because of their completed mission. This is the only time Mark uses the term to describe the Twelve. He usually describes them as learners (disciples). This is also one of the few times when the learners are described in such positive terms. Jesus has called them faithless before, and shortly Mark will describe them as not understanding and having their hearts hardened.

Again, because of the press of the crowds and because of the completed mission, Jesus wants to withdraw and talk with the learners in private. This happens several times in the book (Mark 4:34; 6:32; 7:33; 9:2, 28; 13:3). The people are persistent, however, and privacy evades Jesus once again. Jesus recognizes that the crowd is like a flock of sheep without a shepherd; so He teaches them. The book of Mark is known as an action book that contains little of Jesus' teachings. While the contents of His teaching lessons are missing, the fact that Jesus teaches occurs many times in Mark, just as on this occasion. He teaches with power and authority, but Mark does not tell us anything about the content of His lesson.

The learners of Jesus tell Him about a problem. The crowd has come to hear Jesus on the spur of the moment and are unprepared to stay because they have brought no food. It is late afternoon when the learners suggest that Jesus should send the people away so they can buy food for their evening meal. Jesus' solution to the problem is to have the learners feed the crowds!

The learners are skeptical and ask Jesus whether they should purchase 200 denarii worth of bread (which would require about seven month's wages) to feed the people. Jesus' solution is for the learners to find out how much food is already available. The learners reply that they have five loaves of bread and two fish.

Jesus then instructs the crowd to sit in groups of fifty and one hundred on the green grass. This organizational method is similar to the one used for the encampment of the Israelites before the ark in the wilderness. The green grass indicates that this event took place in the spring, and once again shows the minute details that only an eyewitness would record.

Jesus looked up into heaven, which was an attitude of prayer for Him, and gave a blessing. Contrary to popular thought, Jesus did not bless the bread. It was typical at every Jewish meal that the host would begin the meal with a blessing spoken about God, who provided the food (Deuteronomy 8:10). Thus, God is blessed, not the food. The technical meaning of the word *bless* is to speak well about. Our English word *eulogy* is a transliteration of the Greek word for "speak well about," but is normally translated "to bless." The typical Jewish prayer would be, "Blessed be Thou, Lord God, King of the world, Who has caused bread to come forth out of the earth." There was also a prayer at the end of the meal. Our typical "grace" would be better spoken as a blessing on God for His abundant provision for us.

Having said the blessing, Jesus broke the bread and gave it to the learners to distribute to the crowds. The fish were also divided and given to all. Again, Jesus acts as the head of the house at a normal meal. The blessing, the breaking of a loaf, and its distribution comprised the normal beginning of a Jewish meal. Interestingly, it was also the way Jesus began what we call the Lord's Supper. Everyone ate and was satisfied, and there were twelve baskets of leftovers! The miracle of the multiplication is not explained, but it is clear by the twelve baskets that there was more than enough, not just an ample amount of food. Five thousand men were fed, plus all the women and children who had also been there, but are not specifically mentioned in the text.

Mark shows his church that Jesus is the provider of the staff of life, which is bread. As He provided manna in the wilderness, God, through Jesus, provides bread on this occasion. The real meaning of this miraculous event is not so clearly evident to the crowds but it should have been clear to the learners who had participated so thoroughly in it. But, in a later verse, Mark states that the learners did not understand about the loaves and that their hearts were hardened.

Jesus is the bread of life, not simply physical life, but also spiritual life, and this is the point that the learners missed.

The Calming of the Wind (45-52)

When the five thousand are fed, Jesus compels the learners to get into a boat and cross the sea. He then sends the crowds away, and He himself goes into the hills to pray. Jesus wants to be alone; so He has to dismiss both the crowds and the learners. But when He realizes that the learners are struggling at the oars, Jesus decides to go to them to comfort them. Jesus walks on the water and, according to Mark, intends to go on past them. He apparently wants to encourage them simply by letting them see Him walking on the waves. In bot Psalm 77:19 and Job 9:8, we have pictures of God who rules over the seas in all His power.

67

Seeing Jesus walking on the sea is not a comfort to the learners, however. On the contrary, it is a frightening sight. They think that they have seen a ghost and become very troubled, and cry out, apparently in fear. Jesus speaks to them with a threefold comforting message. "Be of good cheer! It is I! Do not be afraid!" (Mark 6:50, A.T.). Jesus then boards the boat and the wind ceases. Now the learners are exceedingly astonished.

While this incident is similar to the earlier storm on the sea, it is different in several ways. There is no storm in this incident, and the learners are not in any danger. The powerful Jesus appears, walking on water, and the learners are scared. Jesus' words of comfort are also revelatory words because He identifies himself as the great "I Am." Instead of passing by as He planned, He stops and reassures the followers.

We have no further words from Jesus, but Mark makes two interesting comments. The learners did not understand about the loaves, and the hearts of the learners were hardened (Mark 6:52). This verse appears to be out of context because the issue immediately preceding has to do with walking on water, not about bread. Mark's comment about not understanding was used earlier in chapter 4, regarding outsiders who did not accept Jesus. Mark's expression concerning the hardening of hearts was used earlier in reference to the opponents of Jesus.

Why does Mark appear to be so hard in his description of the learners? What does bread have to do with the learner's astonishment about Jesus' walking on the water? It is precisely because the walking-on-water incident is simply another occasion on which the learners do not really know who Jesus is. After they participated in the feeding of five thousand men with only five loaves of bread and two fish, why should they be surprised that Jesus could also walk on the water?

The learners had seen Jesus perform all sorts of healing, yet they did not recognize who He really was. The bread provided by Jesus was really a sign to indicate Jesus' identity, and the learners missed the point entirely. They saw the miracle but missed who really performed the miracle. This Jesus is really from God, and the learners still have not learned that. We marvel also. What is the matter with those thickheads? If we had seen all of Jesus' miracles, we are certain that we would not be surprised at His walking on water or calming the wind—He had even done that before.

For Mark's readers, the learners' denseness could be reassuring. Mark's readers believe in Jesus, and they know about His death and resurrection. The lack of understanding and the learners' hard hearts implies that Mark's audience should not have that problem because they know how the story of Jesus ends. They have a longer perspective of events. They have accepted Jesus as the Son of God. Mark is writing his book to reconfirm that fact for them. Being a follower of Jesus was not easy then and, by implication, is not easy now. The rowing was tough. The "ghost" was frightening, but not real. Jesus was near to reassure them, and is near us by His words, "Be of good cheer; It is I; do not fear" (Mark 6:50, A.T.) Mark's church faced persecution and needed to be reminded of Jesus' presence and power. This incident shows that Jesus is both powerful and present for those who trust Him. Jesus is the bread of life. We should understand that Jesus provides for us today.

Summary of Healings (53-56)

This small section is a summary used by Mark to indicate once more that the popularity and power of Jesus continued in miraculous ways. Jesus is still surrounded by crowds wherever He goes. People who are sick seek simply to touch His clothes to obtain healing, and they are healed. Despite what appears to us as mere superstition, people are healed because of their trust in the power of Jesus. Perhaps this is another way that Mark contrasts the power of the trust of the crowds even when the close followers do not understand and their hearts are hardened. We ought to be very careful, as we attempt to understand God, that we do not miss Him.

CHAPTER SIX

The Son of God!

Mark 7:1—8:30

Conflicts Over Tradition (7:1-23)

This section, concerning uncleanness, appears to be an interlude between healings. It also leads up to the healing of the Syrophoenician woman's daughter, who not only had an unclean spirit, but was also a Gentile, which means she was unclean. Mark lays a foundation to stress the importance of his church's mission to the Gentiles and the probable opposition of Jewish Christians to that mission.

The Pharisees and some scribes from Jerusalem meet with Jesus to discuss the law. (The fact that some scribes came from Jerusalem indicates that Jesus had attracted some attention from the capital.) During their meetings, the Pharisees and scribes see some of Jesus' learners eating bread with common hands. The expression *common* is variously translated "unclean," "profane," or "defiled." Mark explains that the meaning is "unwashed." The concept means that the learners had not ceremonially washed their hands before eating.

Mark explains the Jewish practice of ceremonial washings to his Gentile readers. The washings, or more precisely translated, "immersions," were a part of the traditions of the elders. The ritual immersions included immersing oneself completely after walking and shopping in the markets. The Jews reasoned that, having been in the markets, they probably had touched someone who was unclean and therefore had become unclean. Cleaning their eating utensils was simply an extension of cleaning their hands.

This cleaning ritual was not merely a health precaution as we would understand it today, but for the Pharisee and scribe, it was an extension of the law. They wanted to keep the law as perfectly as possible; so their traditions were built as a kind of additional wall around the law so that they would never break the law. In

Exodus 30:19 and 20, the priests were instructed to wash their hands and feet before entering the tent of meeting. The Pharisees felt they could more exactly keep the law if they were always as ritually clean as the priests. All of these traditions originated from good motives and became a part of the Jewish oral law.

These interpretations were handed down from generation to generation and were called traditions of the elders. Over time, these traditions built up their own authority and became as binding as the original law. Mark describes these first as "tradition of the elders" (Mark 7:3, 5), then as "traditions of men" (Mark 7:8), and finally as "your own traditions" (Mark 7:9). The quotation from Isaiah describes them as "rules taught by men" (Mark 7:7). All these expressions are contrasted to the commands of God.

Because the Pharisees see Jesus' learners eating with ritually unclean hands, they question Jesus: why are His learners not living according to the traditions of the elders? This question by the Pharisees is really a twofold challenge to Jesus. First, to challenge the learner is to challenge the teacher. Second, the Pharisees challenge Jesus' teaching, since He is not teaching the traditions of the elders. In fact, Mark has already noted that Jesus did not teach as the scribes, but as one who had His own authority and not as the elders (Mark 1:22).

Jesus gives three answers to their question. First, He quotes from the Old Testament prophet Isaiah; then He gives a contemporary illustration of what Isaiah means; finally, He directly addresses their question by explaining what real uncleanness concerns.

The quotation from Isaiah 29:13 is from the Septuagint and is a good example of twofold prophecy. Isaiah was speaking directly to Israel, warning them about their current behavior and God's coming judgment. Jesus understands that Isaiah's words are also relevant to His contemporaries and their current behavior. They are, in fact, hypocrites. This is the only place that Mark uses the word *hypocrite*. In Jesus' time, it literally meant an actor, but figuratively it meant someone who was pretending. Israel spoke words but did not mean them. Israel worshiped God, not as God directed, but as they thought best. The Pharisees were duplicating Israel, and unfortunately, we often duplicate the Pharisees. The essence of the meaning of Isaiah's prophecy for Jesus' audience is not left in doubt. Jesus explains that in their fervent endeavor to hold on to the traditions they have built up, they have left the commands of God. There is a later implication that this has been intentional.

Jesus provides the Pharisees with an illustration. He begins by complimenting them on their perversity. Rather sarcastically, Jesus says they have found a good way to set aside God's command so they can keep the traditions they have built up over the years. Again, we see a contrast between the command of God and the traditions they hold. The contrast is between what Moses said and what the Pharisees say. Jesus first gives the commands of God (Mark 7:10); then He shows how they violate those commands with their traditions (Mark 7:11-13).

The first command cited is in the Ten Commandments: "Honor your father and your mother." (See Exodus 20:12.) The second is an explication of the first: "Anyone who curses [speaks evil about] his father or mother must be put to death." (See Exodus 21:17.) In contrast to these, Jesus cites the tradition called "Corban." If an individual decided to give all of his possessions to God, then he declared them "Corban" (gift or offering to God; a cognate of this word is used in Matthew 27:6 as the name of the temple treasury box). In Corban, although the individual kept all of his possessions until his death, he had to use them for sacred rather than ordinary use. This meant he did not have to use them to support his parents. This could be a hasty vow from which a Rabbi may or may not release the individual.

"Corban" was a good practice, but Jesus is making the point that care of parents should take precedence. Human needs and concerns are above good practices. Jesus concludes the illustration by saying that the Pharisees and scribes have "nullified" the word of God by the traditions they handed down to the next generation. The word *nullify* is used in classical Greek as a legal term meaning to cancel a will, which is the effect of Corban in this instance. The traditions that started out as a good attempt to help people keep the law of God had been used by hypocrites to invalidate the word of God. Jesus adds, "You do many things like that" (Mark 7:13). This is not an isolated incident. It is no wonder that Jesus calls them hypocrites (playactors).

Jesus then returns to the issue of uncleanness. He turns from the Pharisees and scribes to the people and asks them to listen carefully and understand what He is about to say: what makes a person "common" (defiled, unclean) is not what goes into him or her in terms of food, even food eaten with unwashed hands; what demonstrates a person's uncleanness is what comes from his or her heart. This principle, stated in Mark 7:15, is an enigmatic statement, and when Jesus leaves and goes into the house, the learners ask Him what He means by this parable (Mark 7:17). The word *parable* here does not mean story, but proverb, or more precisely, a riddle.

Despite Jesus' call to listen carefully and understand, the learners do not understand. Jesus knows this by the nature of their questions, which He now answers. Note here that Jesus' audience changes from the Pharisees and scribes, then to the people, and then to the learners; yet Mark's readers get the information that is directed to all three audiences. Mark's readers should not be in a position to have heard and still not understand.

Jesus is upset that the learners do not understand. Jesus refers to actual food and says that a person eats it and it passes through the stomach and is ultimately expelled; the food never passes through the heart. In contrast, it is the heart that matters; it is what comes from inside that makes a person unclean. What comes from inside a person comes from the heart and shows what he is like inside: that is, whether he is clean or unclean. Mark, in a parenthesis, declares that Jesus teaches that all foods are clean and that food laws are not important because He has nullified these laws. It is at this point that Jesus skips from a discussion of unclean food to His real concern. The condition of a person's heart is the real issue. Just as in the quotation from Isaiah, the heart is far from God, so also the food that goes into the body does not touch the heart: it is what comes out of the heart that really makes a person unclean.

The corrupt heart is a result of bad reasoning, not bad food. Jesus gives a list of twelve matters that demonstrate bad reasoning. The first six are listed in the plural form (although they are not so translated in the NIV) and generally are associated with actions: (1) sexual immoralities, (2) thefts, (3) murders, (4) adulteries, (5) covetings, and (6) evil deeds. Three of these deal with sexual issues: sexual immoralities, which include all sexual sins, not simply what we refer to as fornication; adulteries, which refer especially to incidents of intercourse by married people outside of their marriage vows; and covetings, which should be understood to mean lusting after another person.

The second six bad reasonings, which are all in singular form, illustrate attitudes rather than actions: (1) deceit, (2) lewdness

74

(filthy mouth), (3) evil eye (probably a reference to stinginess—see Deuteronomy 15:9), (4) insults or slander, (5) arrogance, and (6) unthinkingness are reflections of how a person talks. How you talk illustrates what is in your heart, just as much as how you walk (behave) illustrates what is in your heart and what you think is really important. The evil that we do is not a result of what external things are about us, but what has influenced us to decide whether we will be clean or unclean in both thoughts and actions. The source of uncleanness is not things but persons, especially the heart of a person. It is the person who is unclean. This makes moral purity not simply a matter of actions, but also of thoughts.

There are many applications for Mark's readers and for us. It is clear both in Acts and in Paul's letters that Jewish-Gentile conflicts were prominent in the church for some time. (See Acts 10 and 15, as well as Galatians and Romans). Mark intends that his Gentile church should not be attached to the religious traditions that accompanied the Jews who became Christians. Attempts to make human laws into God's law must be opposed. Any time our understanding of God's Word interferes or negates the primary meaning of God's Word, we are in the same position as the Pharisees. Sometimes we also construct a fence around Scripture and increase its laws so that we will not break the primary laws. We must remember to keep the principles of the New Testament but be vigilant that we do not force our interpretations on others as law.

We have many church traditions today (11:00 Sunday morning worship, invitation after every sermon, offerings during the worship services). These traditions probably all had good reasons when they were begun, but are the purposes of God still being served through these traditions? Traditions must always be subservient to the Word of God. Traditions are not in themselves bad, but they can become bad when they become more important than people.

It is very easy for us to blame externals for our troubles. We have all heard the phrase, "The devil made me do it." Jesus says our problem is inside. We need to look at our inner selves first, rather than blame external occurrences or others for our behavior.

Ritual uncleanness is not a problem for us today, but we have kept the distinction between the sacred and the secular. If Jesus declared all foods clean, then He has declared all of His creation clean. Romans 14 makes it clear that it is not the object or action itself that is unclean, but the lack of faith (trust) on the part of the Christian. Our money, lives, houses, jobs, cars, church buildings, and Bibles are neither clean, unclean, secular, or sacred themselves, but only as our heart or trust makes them. "Nothing is unclean in itself, but it is unclean to the one who thinks it unclean" (Romans 14:14, A.T.).

Christians should think of everything as clean or sacred. The printed Bible is a book of paper and ink, but the concepts and words of God written in it are sacred to Christians. The church building is constructed of glass, concrete, metal, and wood, but it becomes a sacred place as we come to worship God in it. The Communion is merely juice and bread, but it becomes holy as we share it in trust. If you have a paid position, your occupation (whether you are an accountant, a pilot, a clerk, a beautician, or a farmer) is sacred or not, depending on your trust. In fact, all of your time should be considered sacred: the times you spend with children, your friends, in retirement, in working around the house, and on vacation are all valuable and God-given. They are sacred.

Healings in Non-Jewish Territories (7:24-37)

A Syrophoenician Woman (24-30)

Jesus retreats again into Gentile territory to escape the crowds. His healings have attracted many people, and while Jesus continues to heal, His real concern is about announcing God's kingdom and teaching His learners. He does not want to be known simply as a healer. But Mark often indicates that although Jesus wants to retreat, the people are usually not far behind. It is true in this incident: Jesus goes north into Gentile territory along the coast of the Mediterranean Sea to the area of Tyre and stays in a home where He hopes the crowd will not locate Him.

However, a woman who has a small daughter with an unclean spirit comes with a request for her daughter's healing. We can presume from her behavior that she has heard about Jesus' power and authority. She has heard that He is able to throw out demons, even when He is not actually present. The woman's request is heightened by her subservient attitude to Jesus. She falls at His feet and pleads for Him to throw the demon out of her daughter.

Mark interrupts his story at this point to explain the woman's background. The woman is a Greek Syrophoenician by birth. This is to help us understand Jesus' reply. Jesus' answer about letting the children be satisfied with food first is an indication of His sense of purpose. Jesus' entry into Gentile territory was not to preach good news to Gentiles, but to get away from the crowds. Jesus' purpose was to let His service be known to the Jews first. He explains to the woman that it is not right to take the children's bread from the table and give it to the small dogs who wait under the table for the scraps.

Some scholars think that Jesus' allusion to children means Israel, and that the mention of dogs means the Gentiles. There is no deep meaning here between the woman and Jesus. Jesus is sitting at a table and His allusion to children, food, and small dogs are consistent with what would have been occurring in many households. The word for dogs is a diminutive form of the word and should be translated "small dogs," or perhaps even "puppies." These are not the normal scavengers that the Old Testament most often mentions. *Small dog* is used in the New Testament only in this passage and in a parallel passage in Matthew 15. The word *dog* is used five times in the New Testament, and every time it has a negative connotation. Despite the fact that Mark is known for using diminutives without purpose, Matthew does not. While Matthew uses *small dogs* in the parallel passage, he does not use the other diminutive forms *(daughter, children,* and *child)* that Mark uses in this passage.

The woman's reply to Jesus demonstrates her humility, persistence, and belief that Jesus can and will do what she asks. Her reply is not to say that Gentiles are not dogs. She does not argue with Jesus, but uses the same allusion to the table and says that even the small dogs underneath the table get the children's crumbs. The woman only wants what may be left over. This is another indication that she has heard of Jesus' compassion and concern for others. Her ready answer as well as her persistence have convinced Jesus. Jesus' answer to the woman is simple and to the point. He tells her that the demon has already left her small daughter. The incident is concluded by Mark's description of the woman's arriving home to find the demon gone and her daughter resting comfortably in bed (Mark 7:30).

This section shows Jesus' active disregard for the clean and unclean prescriptions of the Pharisees as described in the first part of Mark 7. Jesus goes into Gentile (unclean) territory and heals a Gentile (unclean person). If the unclean are now clean as the previous section shows, then Gentiles do have an opportunity, but after the Jews. This is how Mark and his church understand the ministry of Jesus, and this is how Paul describes his ministry. The good news is to go to the Jew first and then to the Gentiles. We today assume that Jesus came for us (Gentiles). The Gentiles of early church times did not make that assumption. Our thinking is wrong. We need to see how the Gentile saw the proclamation of the good news to them: it was a part of the great grace or favor of God.

Mark uses this incident to explain to his Gentile audience why Jesus did not go to the Gentiles. It simply was not Jesus' purpose. "First the children" implies that the Gentiles come after the children. So Mark's Gentile audience is pleased that Jesus takes time to distribute crumbs to those who are under the table. Perhaps we would take a more humble position if we were to realize our Gentile origins. Perhaps it would also encourage us to continue to give testimony to the Jews, who were first.

A Deaf Man in the Decapolis (31-37)

Mark is interested in documenting something of Jesus' actual travel route; thus He notes Jesus' circuitous path from Tyre to the Decapolis. But by making this distinction, Mark indicates that Jesus is again in Gentile territory, where the unclean live.

A man is brought to Jesus who is both deaf and has some speaking impediment. The word that indicates his speaking impediment occurs in Scripture only here and in Isaiah 35:6. The Isaiah passage describes the wonderful deliverance of Zion. Mark has in mind that this man will be delivered. Mark wants his readers to know that Jesus is the one who not only delivers this man from deafness, but will also deliver his readers because Jesus does all things well. The request to have Jesus set His hands on the man is a typical request for healing or blessing.

Jesus is still concerned about privacy; so He takes the man away from the crowd, and after the healing, He will tell the man not to tell anyone. Then Jesus groans in the process of healing the man. While the groaning may come because any healing is a battle with the devil, it may also be another indication of Jesus' frustration at His inability to keep a low profile. Jesus also knows that this healing will mean more publicity and more crowds will come.

All this happens when Jesus has constantly wanted to be alone with His learners.

Mark shows that exactly the opposite of what Jesus wants occurs. Jesus gives orders to people not to tell to anyone what has happened, but the more He gives orders, the more they announce the news. Jesus wants His power and authority veiled during His earthly service so He can continue to teach and preach. Mark, however, wants the power and authority of Jesus announced; so he illustrates how the people continued to proclaim what Jesus did for them despite His command to be silent. If the ones who were told by Jesus to keep silent were unable to do so, how much more should we, who are told to proclaim the good news, tell it! Yet the fact is that they told when they were not supposed to tell, and quite often we do not tell even though Jesus has told us to go into all the world and preach the good news.

The healing account is rich with detail. A close verbal account is indicated by the details of Jesus' fingers in the man's ears, the spit, the touching of the tongue, and Jesus' Aramaic word of healing. The ears of the man are opened and the chain of his tongue is loosened. Jesus words, "Be opened completely," refer not simply to the ears but to the tongue and to the whole life. The result of the healing is that the man can now speak correctly; he no longer has a speaking impediment. The man was never "deaf and dumb" (a better term is speechless), but had grown deaf and then lost his ability to speak clearly as a result of his inability to hear.

The crowd is astounded. The point of the story for Mark's audience is that Jesus is a person who does all things well. Jesus, just as Isaiah predicted, brings hearing to the deaf and speech to those who have an impediment. Jesus does all things well, even for Mark and his church. He also does all things well for us; His power and authority are clearly evident in His service. His power and authority should still be clearly evident in the church today.

Feeding of Four Thousand (8:1-21)

The feeding of the four thousand appears in a similar context to the feeding of the five thousand. After both events, Jesus conflicts with the Pharisees, and He heals the deaf and blind. The culmination of the first series is in the expression, "He has done all things well" (Mark 7:37, A.T.). The culmination of the second is in Peter's confession that Jesus is the Son of God (Mark 8:29).

Another major theme in chapters 6 through 8 concerns bread. Mark has twenty-two references to bread in his book; nineteen of the twenty-two occur in these chapters. There are several references in the feedings, but bread is also mentioned in the controversy about eating bread with unwashed hands, in Jesus' comment to the Syrophoenician woman about the children's bread, and in the discussion with the learners about the leaven of the Pharisees and their concern for the lack of bread.

The feeding of the crowds with bread and fish is a major event for Mark, and he uses both events to indicate to his readers the power and authority of Jesus. However, there is no indication that the people who are present at the event trust: the Pharisees continue to ask for a sign, and the learners do not understand the implications of Jesus' being able to feed five thousand and four thousand people.

There are enough differences in the original text to indicate that there were two separate feeding events:

Five Thousand	Four Thousand
Jesus is approached by learners	Jesus initiates concern
Five loaves and two fish	Seven loaves and few fish
Sat down in companies (50s and 100s)	Sat down
Twelve baskets left over	Seven mat baskets left over

But the result, at least for the learners, was the same at both events. They do not understand about the bread and their hearts are hardened (Mark 6:52; 8:17). Since there were two feeding events, why did the learners ask Jesus in the second situation how one could feed so many people with bread in the desert? First, we do not know the time lapse difference, but apparently the learners did not think that feeding crowds in the desert was a regular feature of Jesus' service; so they did not presume that He would feed the crowd again. But Jesus takes the same action as before by blessing God for the bread and having the learners distribute it. In this event, He also gives thanks to God for the fish before the learners distribute it. Again, the hunger of the crowd is satisfied and there is food left over. The significance of this event for the learners and Mark's audience is made clear in Mark 8:14-21. See that section for further comment.

The Pharisees appear as the opponents of Jesus in this section. They argue, seek a sign, and test Him. The Pharisees are not present to gain information or obtain help, and they are not disinterested officials: they are there to stop Jesus. They try to stop Him through legal arguments but receive no satisfaction; so they decide to ask for a sign from Heaven. It is not unusual to ask for a sign from someone who claims to be a spokesman for God. The sign the Pharisees ask for is not another healing or feeding, but a sign from Heaven that will be a guarantee that what Jesus does and teaches is really from God. The Pharisees want a catastrophic event to demonstrate that Jesus is God's spokesman. The fact that they must ask for a sign demonstrates their unbelief.

This is described by Mark also as a testing of Jesus by the Pharisees. If Jesus does not present some sign from Heaven, then the Pharisees can tell the people that Jesus is a false spokesman: one who cannot be verified, since Jesus cannot, or will not, perform the sign they request.

Jesus is totally exasperated by their request. He groans intensely in His spirit. Why does He have to endure such unbelief? Why does this generation want a sign? Jesus says rather emphatically that no sign will be given. The emphasis is clear because He begins with the Aramaic *amen,* meaning, "Attention: what I am about to say is both true and important." The emphasis is clear because Jesus groans at their lack of belief, and because the language of the sentence reflects a strong Hebrew oath to the negative. Jesus is saying that there is no way that this generation will get the sign for which they are asking. Note the passive voice of the verb: "be given." The sign does not come from Jesus anyway: the sign must come from God. Jesus has demonstrated His power and authority numerous times. These demonstrations were not signs, or at least their *sign* ificance was not apparent to either the Pharisees or the learners. The earlier examples of Jesus' power were not incontrovertible, but they were demonstrations at least to those who trusted.

We often think about having signs today. If we could have a sign from Heaven, we think we would pray more often, do more good works, preach, and evangelize. But if Jesus had given an absolutely convincing sign to the Pharisees, so that they had no alternative but to acknowledge Jesus as God's Son, where would the role of faith (trust) be? An absolute sign would mean walking by sight and not by trust. The very fact that the Pharisees were testing Jesus was an indication of their lack of trust. There will not be an incontrovertible sign given to us. We must build on the demonstrations of God's power in Jesus' life and walk by trust and not by sight. Mark's church—or our church—does not need further signs. If enough has not been demonstrated already to us, then we are in the same condition as the Pharisees. We should be very careful not to be found testing God by asking for further signs.

After the confrontation with the Pharisees, the learners leave the shore and are alone again with Jesus. They have forgotten to bring food, including bread. When Jesus warns them against the yeast of the Pharisees and Herod, the learners worry about not having enough bread and miss Jesus' warning about hypocrisy. Yeast is most often a symbol of evil or corruption that spreads insidiously among the people and places where it grows. The yeast of the Pharisees is identified in Matthew as their teaching. Jesus is warning the learners against the Pharisaic teaching that promotes hypocrisy. The Pharisees had seen Jesus and had witnessed both His power and His authority in feeding, healing, teaching, and throwing out demons, and yet they ask for a sign. The yeast of Herod is also hypocrisy. Herod executed John the Baptist despite the fact that he liked John (Mark 6:20) and believed that John was a right and holy man. Herod heard John gladly even though his teaching was perplexing. Herod, like the Pharisees, was looking for a sign (Luke 23:8). Herod knew better, but he still had John executed.

Jesus leaves the warning unexplained to the learners. He lectures them because they are ignoring His words and worrying about bread, which also means they have ignored His works in multiplying the bread for four thousand and the five thousand. The learners have not understood the meaning of the feedings even when they saw and participated in them. They did not see the *sign*ificance of those feedings. Jesus becomes very harsh with them. As Mark indicated earlier, Jesus is astonished at their lack of understanding (Mark 4:13). This time, Jesus asks several demanding questions without even giving them a chance to answer.

Why do you dispute with each other about bread?

Do you not yet understand?

Do you not yet perceive?

Are your hearts hardened?

Having eyes do you not see?

Having ears do you not hear?

The first question is rhetorical and does not expect an answer. The next two questions and the last two questions are really the same question, all of them framed so that the answer is negative. And the answer to the question about their hearts is an implied yes. The learners have really missed the point. They are described by Mark as being in the same position as the Pharisees and outsiders. The learners' concern about bread is an indication that they have not seen the *sign*ificance behind Jesus' feedings and healings. In fact, they are in the same position as the Pharisees, except the Pharisees are threatened and battle Jesus, while the learners keep trying to understand. Jesus can open ears and heal blind eyes, but is unsuccessful with His learners. Trust cannot be coerced.

Jesus, however, does not give up on the learners. He asks them some questions that are intended to make them think about the facts, and He encourages them to understand the meaning behind them. After feeding five thousand with five loaves, how much was left over? The learners reply, "Twelve baskets." After feeding four thousand with seven loaves, how much was left over? The learners reply, "Seven baskets."

And then the final question, "Do you still not understand?" This final question is left without answer. The learners know the facts but not their significance: Jesus has the power and authority of God! The feeding is not important in itself but only as a sign of who Jesus really is: God, in Jesus, is among them. Mark's audience and we are aware of the facts of Jesus' life, including what the learners did not know at the time (His death, burial, and resurrection). Knowing the facts and understanding and living by them are two different matters, both for the learners and for us.

Mark wants his readers to understand. If the learners did not understand, it is also possible that some of Mark's readers, even though they knew the facts, still did not understand. Mark wants his readers to see Jesus as more than a miracle worker, but as the Son of God who is able to supply bread and is also able to open our eyes and ears to His significance in our lives.

Healing the Blind (8:22-26)

Mark narrates the healing of the blind man as a comparison to the healing of the deaf man in chapter 7. Note the similarities:

Deaf	**Blind**
Brought to Jesus by others	Brought to Jesus by others
Jesus takes man aside	Jesus takes man out of village
Spit is used	Spit is used
Man speaks correctly	Man sees clearly
Do not tell others	Go home, do not go into village

Mark has set the deaf incident as the conclusion of a series with a statement of praise for Jesus because He does all things well. The incident of the blind man is also the conclusion of a series, and it ends with Peter's confession that Jesus is the Christ. There are two other important connections. As was discussed during the Mark 7:31-37 passage, a sign of the in-breaking God's deliverance for Israel is the healing of the blind and deaf (Isaiah 35:5, 6). Jesus' healings of the blind and deaf are not important in themselves, but they are signs of who Jesus really is: the Christ of God.

These two incidents also remind the readers that Jesus had just questioned the learners about having eyes that do not see and ears that do not hear (Mark 8:18). Perhaps the meaning of the gradual healing of the blind man is that the learners are also blind but that Jesus will gradually heal their blindness so that they will come to recognize who He really is.

The healings Jesus performed are not signs that compel belief. Jesus did not want to be known only as a healer because that would bring more crowds who would only want to be healed. Healings are a sign of the power and authority of Jesus and are not as important in themselves as they are important signs to indicate to all who Jesus really is.

Jesus Is the Son of God (8:27-30)

This section is the center of Mark's good news. Up to this point, the learners have not learned who Jesus is. The readers know because Mark told them in the title of his book that he was writing good news about Jesus Christ, the Son of God. This section is the middle of Mark's Gospel, and Jesus is again identified as the Christ. Mark reports in the concluding pages of his book that the centurion exclaims at Jesus' death that this man really was the Son of God. Thus, the book is framed in beginning, middle, and end with the fact that Jesus is the Son of God.

This section is also the turning point for the book, because from this time on, Jesus tries to teach His learners that His Christ-hood means suffering, death, and resurrection. Up to this point, power and authority are seen in Jesus' healing and teaching. After this point, the nature and purpose of Jesus as the Christ, the Son of God on earth, is not to demonstrate power and authority through healings and other miracles, but to allow himself to be captured, killed, and after three days to rise from the dead. Jesus says this three times on the way to Jerusalem for those very events (Mark 8:31—10:52). After the third prediction, Jesus begins His last week in Jerusalem, which leads to the fulfillment of His prediction concerning His own death, burial, and resurrection. Each prediction is met with dismay by the learners, and Jesus tries to teach them what true Christhood is all about. The Christhood of Jesus is not that of a popular earthly king who conquers all enemies and makes Israel a world power as in David's time. This Davidic Christ is rejected by Jesus.

This first prediction event is set several miles north of Bethsaida in the country around the major city Caesarea Philippi. Caesarea Philippi was north of the Sea of Galilee and outside of most Jewish influence and populace. Jesus goes here to escape the crowds and remains in the small villages rather than in the city itself.

Since the question of whether the learners understand and the question is unanswered (Mark 8:21), Mark supplies a partial answer in the incident on the road between villages. Yes, someone does understand, or at least knows the correct words, even if that one might not understand their implication. Jesus asks two contrasting questions. First, "Who do people say I am?" (Mark 8:27). The learners answer this question with the same names that were mentioned when Herod wondered who Jesus was (Mark 6:14, 15). Some think Jesus is John the Baptist revived. Herod thought that. Others think that Jesus is Elijah either revived or the Elijah that Malachi predicted would precede the Christ (Malachi 4:5). Others think that Jesus is one of the prophets.

Note that there is no talk about Jesus' being the promised Christ. The Pharisees had asked John the Baptist if he were the Christ. There were several false Christs known to have made claims to Christhood, but the popular opinion about Jesus does not include this concept. Jesus, even though He was extremely popular, did not appear to the people to be the Christ that they expected. Jesus is not recognized by anyone as the Christ, the Son of God; only the voice from Heaven at His baptism and the demons whom Jesus commanded to be quiet know who He is.

The second question Jesus asks His learners concerns who they (as opposed to the crowds) think He is. The answer is given by Peter, who acts as a spokesman for the learners. Peter states that Jesus is not the one who prepares the way as John the Baptist declared himself to be or as the people expected Elijah to be; Jesus is not simply one of the prophets that God sends to bring His message to the people; Jesus is the Christ. *Christ* is a transliteration of the Greek word *anointed,* just as *Messiah* is a transliteration of the Aramaic. The anointed one of God is the one who has been set aside by anointing with oil for a special task. Priests and kings were anointed with oil and set apart for their special task.

But the promised Christ was prophet, priest, and king. The problem for the people in Jesus' time is that their expectations of what the Christ would be and do are far different from what Jesus actually does. So they do not recognize Him despite His healings and miracles. As mentioned previously, Jesus tries to explain to His learners what being Christ really means while He travels to Jerusalem to fulfill His predictions concerning His own suffering, death, and resurrection.

Jesus tells the learners not to tell anyone what He has told them. The command not to tell implies that Jesus accepts Peter's statement. There are two probable reasons that Jesus has for silence concerning His Christhood. First, if the learners were to start proclaiming Jesus as the Christ, Jesus probably would never get to Jerusalem—the Jewish leaders in Galilee would have Him killed. But more probable is that the learners do not really understand what Peter has just said. Christhood, to them, means earthly power and dominion. This is demonstrated by Peter (the one who spoke for the learners and acknowledges that Jesus is the Christ) when he rebukes Jesus for saying that the Christ must be rejected and killed. Mark uses the next several incidents to show the true nature and purpose of the Christ, that is, His death, burial, and resurrection.

Part Two

Jesus Teaches the True Nature
and Purpose of His Sonship

Mark 8:31—10:52

CHAPTER SEVEN

Frightening Predictions
Mark 8:31—9:32

The First Prediction of Jesus' Death (8:31—9:1)

Peter and Jesus Rebuke Each Other (31-33)

Immediately after Peter's profession that Jesus is the Christ, Jesus begins to teach His learners the real meaning of Sonship or Christhood. This proves to be an extremely difficult task. While Jesus' teaching on His death and resurrection begins in this section, Mark mentions this same teaching by Jesus two more times before it actually happens.

Jesus says that it is necessary for the Son of Man to suffer many things, to be disapproved by the Jewish leaders, to be killed, and to rise again after three days. Jesus teaches that this is the way that God has commanded, and therefore it is the only way. The expression *Son of Man* occurs earlier in Mark 2:10 and 28, but in those two passages the expression is basically a substitute for the personal pronoun *I*. The remaining eleven times the expression occurs in Mark are in the later half of the book, after the turning point (Mark 8:27-30). Three of these times are in the three teaching occasions when Jesus is trying to explain to His learners that He will be killed and rise on the third day. Five of the times are references to the same suffering under the Jewish rulers in Jerusalem, which includes His betrayal, scourging, and crucifixion. The other three times are references to the coming Son of Man in power and great splendor (Mark 8:38; 13:26; 14:62).

Thus, *Son of Man* has three different meanings, depending upon the context in which the phrase occurs. It can either be used as a substitute for the pronoun *I* or it has the contrasting meanings of Jesus as the suffering Son of Man or the returning triumphant Son of Man. The Daniel 7:13 Scripture, so well known in Jesus' time as a possible Messianic reference, alludes to

89

the triumphant Son of Man. However, Daniel 7:21 alludes to the Son of Man as servant. The term is almost exclusively used by Jesus as a reference to himself. It was probably a preferable term since the expression *Christ* was so misunderstood.

Jesus was to suffer many things. Isaiah 53 records the concept of a suffering servant, but Judaism had never applied this passage to the expected Christ. Jesus is aware that He will be betrayed, tried, scourged, and mocked before He is killed. The rejection, or more accurately, the disapproval, was voiced by the Sanhedrin, composed of the elders, chief priests, and scribes. This supreme court of Israel listened to Jesus and rejected/disapproved His claim. They turned Him over to the Gentile authorities to be killed. But Jesus also claimed that He would rise again after three days. Hosea 6:2 speaks about God's raising up Israel after two days and after three days because they have decided to return to the Lord. This passage was later interpreted by the Jews as God's promise to revive them, but prophetically it is a reference to Jesus' resurrection.

This section and the other two sections of Jesus' teaching about His death and resurrection include the essence of the good news: Jesus died, He was buried, and He was raised on the third day. This is the good news in the preaching in Acts, and it is the identical summary of the good news that Paul gives in 1 Corinthians 15:3f. It is the same good news formula that we know. Jesus died for our sins, was buried, and resurrected to demonstrate a life after death.

Mark mentions that Jesus spoke these words very plainly or clearly. Mark sees the profession of Peter as the turning point of the book. From this point, Jesus plainly sets before His learners the ultimate fate of His life on earth. Jesus starts for Jerusalem. Jesus has selected the way of the cross, not the way of the power and glory of the world.

Even though Jesus spoke very clearly, His prediction could only be understood after the fact. This is the reason Peter does not understand. Not only is the concept of the Christ as a suffering Christ outside of Peter's ability to comprehend, but knowing Jesus' ability to perform miracles would certainly have prevented Peter from understanding Jesus' death at the hands of Jewish leaders.

Peter takes Jesus aside and begins to explain to Him that He must be wrong. Jesus, aware that His learners are watching, turns and tells Peter that he is wrong. Peter's rebuke was intended to be personal, but Jesus' rebuke of Peter is public for the sake of the learners. The strong expression, "Go off after me, Adversary" (Mark 8:33, A.T.), indicates that Jesus saw Peter's rebuke as a temptation or pressure to take an easier way, or perhaps even to disobey God. Jesus puts Peter into his proper place when He tells Peter to get behind Him. The word *behind* literally means after, and is used by Mark in the sense of "to come after Jesus," that is, "to follow Jesus." Peter's rebuke is an attempt to usurp Jesus' leadership; so Jesus tells Peter, in effect, "Do not try to lead Me; you follow after Me." The word *satan* is better translated "adversary." Peter is seen as the adversary because he attempts to lead Jesus instead of being His follower, and Jesus informs him of the fact.

Jesus speaks about Peter's reasoning as shortsighted because Peter thinks in the manner of men and not in the manner of God. Our problem is also that of gaining the correct perspective. The correct perspective is God's perspective, but we find it difficult to see. Jesus' explanation about how we might gain that perspective by denying ourselves, saying yes to God and accepting His perspective, is explained in Mark's next section. Peter's profession in Mark's earlier section is significant, but because he does not understand its implication, Peter makes the gross error of rebuking Jesus. Our acknowledgment of Jesus as the Christ does not mean that we have achieved perfection either. After our acknowledgment, we still must deny ourselves, take up the cross and follow.

Jesus Teaches Self-denial (8:34 — 9:1)

As Jesus turns towards the learners to rebuke Peter, He summons both the crowd and His learners to hear His answer concerning how one can think the things of God rather than the things of men. Jesus begins with the conditional clause, "If anyone would come after me, . . ." (Mark 8:34). Just as He told Peter to come after Him and not to try to lead Him, Jesus invites anyone to come after Him.

The condition is followed by three commands: (1) "Let that one thoroughly deny himself" (A.T., as also the following quotations). Literally, this means to say no to oneself and yes to God. One cannot serve self and God. The learners need to know that following Jesus does not mean world dominion; it is not an ego trip. To follow Jesus is not to earn the best position in the kingdom, but it is to serve others, just as Jesus did. Note that the action is voluntary. Those who decide to come after Jesus must voluntarily deny themselves.

Jesus continues: (2) "Let that one take up his cross." The cross, to Jesus' audience, was an instrument of Roman execution, though it was seldom used in their area. It was a particularly painful death. The one being executed had to carry the cross beam of the cross to the execution ground. Obviously, the condemned did not go voluntarily; so it seemed incongruous that anyone should voluntarily take up a cross. Mark's readers knew about crucifixions in Rome because Nero had created a spectacle of burning Christians after the fire of Rome. Jesus' command to take up the cross would be especially difficult for the Christians in Mark's audience to accept since they lived in Rome.

The final admonition: (3) "Let that one follow Me." Jesus was just beginning to teach His learners what following meant. The learners were to see shortly that following Jesus was not the road to glory and a mighty earthly kingdom, but a humiliating road to mockery, false trial, and death. Mark's audience already knows that following Jesus means death, but He also is trying to make them understand that while following is both humiliation and service, it is also ultimate glory.

The people who read Mark today can come to understand the concept of self-denial, especially that following Jesus means serving others and considering others before oneself. It is the idea of the cross that is difficult for us to accept as a command for the learner. We falsely assume that we have a cross to bear if we have to live with a heavy burden because of our, or someone else's, mistakes. But remember that Jesus voluntarily took up the cross. Physical persecution is not prevalent in America today. I am not certain that Jesus, or Mark, had mental or emotional persecution in mind. The cross is also a symbol of service: we as followers of Jesus can readily take up the cross of service daily, but only as we forget (deny) ourselves.

The commands of Mark 8:34 are explained in Mark 8:35-38. Verses 35 and 38 utilize allusions to court trials, which were to become a reality to Jesus shortly, and were a reality to Mark's church. To exclaim in court that you do not accept Christ in the attempt to save your physical life is really a form of destroying or losing your life because you are ashamed of Jesus and His words. The person who is taken to court and gives testimony to Christ and the good message may well lose physical life, but will gain eternal life when the Son of Man comes in the splendor of the Father. Verse 35 contrasts losing the soul with saving the soul, while verse 38 contrasts the adulterous and sinful generation with the time when the Son of Man comes in the splendor of the Father with the holy angels.

Verses 36 and 37 utilize business allusions in the form of rhetorical questions. *Benefit* (NIV has *good*) and *exchange* are commerce and trade terms. The implied answer to these questions is that there is no benefit to gain the world and lose the soul, and that there is nothing that a person can give in exchange for his soul. *Soul* here has the Hebrew meaning of the whole of a person's life and not simply one's spiritual being.

Mark gives concrete examples in the process of explaining the three commands for his church audience. He shows that following Jesus as the Son of Man who will be mocked, tried, and executed also means being with the Son of Man when He comes in the splendor of the Father. Here is the contrast between the functions of the Son of Man: the unexpected Son of Man who gives His life as a ransom must come first, before the glorious Son of Man comes in magnificent power. This is a part of the mystery and secret of the kingdom: triumph comes through rejection, trial, and crucifixion. What a mighty comfort for Mark's church! They may also have to suffer trial, rejection, and death; but triumph awaits those who endure to the end.

Mark 9:1 is a continuation of the concept of the ultimate triumph. The kingdom of God coming in power is both a reference to the Son of Man's coming in power (Mark 8:38), but also a reference to the power the three learners will see shortly in the transfiguration of Jesus. The transfiguration is a proleptic figure of Jesus' coming resurrection and ultimate second coming in splendor, both of which are further examples of His triumph.

Transfiguration Declares Jesus as Son of God (9:2-13)

The specific time reference to six days (Mark 9:2) is an allusion to verse 1, where Jesus says that some will not taste death until they see the kingdom of God coming in power. The transformation of Jesus helps the learners understand that Jesus, though He predicts suffering and death, is still the Son of Man who has both power and glory, as witnessed by this transformation.

Jesus is with His learners. Peter, James, and John are often described as the inner three and get special attention: Mark described the three men as the only ones Jesus selected to be with Him when He raised Jairus' daughter; Jesus also asks these men to pray with Him in the Garden of Gethsemane; they (with Andrew) ask Jesus concerning the signs of the end of the time; and Mark places the three men together in the list in which the delegates are called. Other lists in Matthew and Luke put Andrew after Simon Peter and before James and John. It is evident that an inner circle existed among the Twelve, composed of Peter, James and John. Andrew, the brother of Peter, is not part of the inner circle but seems to be closer than the rest of the delegates. The others, except for Judas, are rarely if ever mentioned, even in Acts.

Jesus takes the three along with Him to a high hill. Mark emphasizes that they went privately, and the four of them were alone (Mark 9:2). He says that Jesus was literally transformed in front of their eyes. Matthew and Luke tell us His face was changed and brightened. All three accounts mention that His clothes glistened: the whiteness of His clothing refers to the Heavenly origin of the person wearing them (cf. Daniel 7:9; Revelation 3:5; 4:4; 7:9).

Then Elijah and Moses appeared to them. Mark names Elijah first while Matthew and Luke mention Moses first. While the emphasis differs, the two represent the Law and the Prophets. Elijah, a major figure in the Old Testament, was a forerunner of the Messiah in popular Jewish thought. Jesus was mistaken for Elijah by the people who reported to Herod when Herod was disturbed by Jesus' appearance. Jesus is thought to be Elijah by some when Jesus asks the learners who people think He is. Others think that John the Baptist is Elijah, and Jesus equates John with Elijah as the one who precedes the Messiah, although John himself denies it. Crowds mistake Jesus' cry from the cross as a cry for Elijah's help. Jewish popular thought held that Elijah did not die (2 Kings 2:11). He was expected to return and be a forerunner of the Messiah. Malachi 4:5 and 6 prophesied that Elijah would come before the day of the Lord and that he would restore the hearts of Israel. When John the Baptist appeared in the desert preaching repentance, the Jewish leaders sent to question him asked him whether he was Elijah (John 1:21).

The fact that Elijah and Moses left Jesus standing alone is as significant as their appearance with Him. Jesus is the authority for Mark's church. Moses and Elijah are no longer forerunners because the Son of Man has come. The Law and the Prophets are complete now that Jesus, the Son of God, has come: Jesus supersedes Elijah and Moses. This was the clear intent of the disappearance of Moses and Elijah. The pair had accomplished their task of being the forerunners of Christ.

This point was not understood, however, as indicated by Peter's intent to set up three tents to commemorate the event. Every occurrence of the word *tent* in the New Testament, except Hebrews 11:9, is a reference to a religious site. Erection of a tent was like setting up a altar to remember an important event. Mark, in a brief explanation of Peter's improper suggestion, says that Peter mentioned this idea because he did not know what else to say and he was afraid. This explanation is more evidence that Mark received much of his material from Peter, who had good recollection of the event.

The cloud that overshadows them and the voice from the cloud are indications of God's presence and revelation. The word *overshadowed* is used in a similar manner in Luke 1:35, a reference to the birth of Jesus, and in Acts 5:15, a reference to miraculous healings as Peter's shadow falls on people. The voice from the cloud, like the voice in Mark 1:11, affirms that Jesus is the Son of God. The learners are not only to acknowledge that, but they should listen to Him.

The whole event is a continuation of Mark's theme that Jesus is the Son of God. It is also an affirmation that Jesus will be resurrected, and they also will be resurrected. The whole process is for the learner's benefit: to teach them that Jesus is the Son of Man glorified, even though He has just told them that He is the Son of Man soon to suffer mockery, pain, and death. The strengthening of the learners in this event is also meant as a strengthening of Mark's readers who have accepted Jesus as the Son of God and are going through persecution at the present time. Suffering is not the end; there is a resurrection. There is ultimate victory over death and an eternal life with God.

Up to this point in Jesus' service, His commands to be silent are absolute even though they are ignored. This time, Jesus tells the learners that they are to be silent until after the Son of Man has risen from the dead. Jesus is teaching them concerning the real nature of His Christhood. The learners are not to tell about this event until after the resurrection because only then will they have the full story (although Jesus has actually already told them the full story) and have experienced it. After the resurrection, the learners will be able to proclaim Jesus as the Son of Man who both suffered and died but was also resurrected. This is a correction to the learners' current thought that the Son of Man can only be glorified.

The learners knew about and accepted the concept of resurrection. What they did not understand was the connection between the Son of Man and resurrection; to them it was unthinkable that the Son of Man could die. They keep silent although they debate the concept among themselves. They ask Jesus about Elijah because they apparently connect resurrection and the end of time when they consider the prophecy concerning Elijah, who was to come as a forerunner of the end.

Jesus relates the sequence of Elijah's coming, but He says that it is not the end because the Son of Man must suffer and be humiliated. (Jesus emphasizes this because it is at this point that the learners stumble.) He says that Elijah has come and identifies John the Baptist with Elijah. This forerunner, John the Baptist, was persecuted just as Elijah had been persecuted. Jesus cites Elijah again (who had come as John the Baptist and suffered and died) to explain to the learners about the Son of Man and death. The point is that even as Elijah (John the Baptist) suffered, so also suffering is a part of the service of the Son of Man.

The paradox of the suffering Son of Man and the glorified Son of Man disturbs the learners. Jesus shows that both are true: in prediction that emphasizes suffering (Mark 8:31); in prediction that emphasizes glorious coming (Mark 8:38); in transformation, which emphasizes glory; and again in this section, emphasizing the suffering of the Son of Man. The identity of Jesus as the Son of Man is also clear. The rest of Mark emphasizes the Son of Man as suffering.

If it were not for our long association of the idea of the Son of God's suffering, we would have the same problem. Consider how ridiculous the idea would be to most people outside of an awareness of Christianity. God suffering? How preposterous! Mark's church thought this way. We want to follow a victorious leader, not one who is humiliated by mockery and execution. The cross is a paradox. We have become used to the idea of the cross when it no longer carries shame and humiliation. The original concept of the cross as an instrument of death is muted once we wear one that is gold plated for jewelry. (Would we wear a gold plated electric chair trinket for personal adornment? The concept is similar.)

Jesus Throws Out a Stubborn Demon (9:14-29)

Jesus and the inner three return from their mountain experience of seeing Jesus' splendor. They meet His learners and the crowds of people who are arguing because of a lack of trust and an incident of demon possession. Jesus finds His other learners in a dispute with the scribes. We are not told what the dispute concerns, but apparently it is over their failure to throw out the bad spirit from a boy. The crowd plays a major role in this incident because they are listening to the dispute. The crowd first sees Jesus and runs to Him, anticipating that He will settle the dispute. The father of the boy who is possessed speaks to Jesus from the crowd. An even greater crowd has gathered around Jesus just before He heals the boy and then retires to teach His learners in private.

The boy who is possessed is described at length. The father describes the boy as having an unspeaking spirit. The spirit takes over the child and tears at him, apparently hoping to destroy the boy. The boy foams, grinds his teeth, and stiffens up as though he is dead. This has all the appearances of an episode of epilepsy, except that the father says that the boy cannot speak. The spirit in the boy reacts to Jesus' presence by convulsing the boy; he rolls around on the ground and foams. The spirit's evilness is further described by the father; it tries to throw the boy into fire or into water to destroy him. As Jesus throws the spirit out of the boy, the spirit gives one last attempt to destroy the boy by convulsing him once again. This leaves the boy limp as though he were dead. There is no lengthier description of an illness in the New Testament. Mark's description shows the fierce hold this spirit has had on the child; the tenacity of the bad spirit made it difficult for the learners to throw it out.

The learners had been asked to throw out this spirit, but they were not strong enough. They had tried but failed, and they were concerned about their failure. They had been successful before; why did they fail now? They ask Jesus when they are alone with Him. (Jesus had already answered the question, but they had not noticed.) Jesus calls them an unbelieving generation. This is a reference to the learners, not to the crowds. The learners cannot throw out the spirit because they have a lack of trust; they depend upon themselves to throw out the spirit, not upon God.

Jesus explained to them privately that this kind of spirit could only be thrown out by prayer. The learners had not used that method; they had depended upon themselves and their past success. The learners had the power to throw out the spirit (Mark 6:7), but it was apparently not an absolute power. They still had to depend upon God for the power. Prayer was needed because prayer is an acknowledgment of dependence on God.

Jesus castigates them for their lack of trust again. Jesus' exasperation is clear in His rhetorical questions: "How long will I be with you? How long must I endure you?" (Mark 9:19, A.T.). Despite His exasperation, and the disappointment and lack of trust on the learners part, Jesus continues to teach them about himself and His true mission.

The father describes his child's condition to Jesus and pleads for His compassion and help, if Jesus is able. (The father knows the learners were not able; so he is unsure that the teacher is able.) "What do you mean, 'If you are able?'" Jesus repeats, and then He replies, "All things are possible to the one trusting." The father immediately cries out, "I trust; help me in my lack of trust" (Mark 9:23, 24, A.T.).The father believes, but knowing that he also has a lack of belief, he asks for additional help. He is desperate for his son. Even in the face of a little trust, Jesus is able to throw out the spirit from the boy who was in a death-like trance as a result of his convulsion.

This incident demonstrates again Jesus' healing power, especially against such a powerful spirit. Mark contrasts the splendor of Jesus on the mountain with the evil that lies close at hand. Jesus is still the Son of God in power. Jesus takes tragedy and turns it into triumph.

The most valuable application of this text to us concerns trust. First, we ought never to take our ability to live for granted. We must live by trust. Jesus says that all things are possible to the one trusting. Our predicament is the same as the father's; we trust, but we also have a lack of trust, and so we need help for our lack of trust. None of us trusts enough, but Jesus says, "Nothing is impossible." Mark's church members, in the face of persecution, needed to say individually, "I trust; help my lack of trust." When we meet daily problems, sorrows, obstacles, and even persecution, we also need to say, "Lord, I trust; help my lack of trust."

Second Prediction of Jesus' Death (9:30-32)

Jesus' patience is evident when He explains a second time to His learners what He is about to experience in Jerusalem. The setting is private because the mission of Jesus' death and resurrection is not to be known until it has been accomplished. But Jesus wants His learners to be prepared; so He takes them aside privately to discuss the coming events.

This prediction has the same basic elements as the first. The Son of Man will be given over to men who will kill Him, but three days after His death, He will rise again. These predictions are identical in content to the good news preached by the apostles and others in the rest of the New Testament. The gospel (good news) is that Jesus was killed and, after three days, rose again.

After the first prediction, Peter was sharply rebuked. This time, no learner responds to Jesus' remarks. They do not understand Him, and since Peter had received such a sharp rebuke earlier, they are afraid to ask any questions. Mark shows in strong contrast the paradox of the transformed Son of God and healer who will be betrayed and killed, but will rise again. Jesus is still teaching the true nature of His mission.

Jesus' death will not be an accident. Jesus teaches the learners that His death is a part of the purpose and plan of God. The learners hear the word *death* and understand it, but they do not understand about a resurrection from the dead (cf. Mark 9:10). This is a part of the problem in Mark's church. They see death ahead because of their persecution, but resurrection is not a reality to them. Mark is trying to assure his audience, and us, that although death is a fearsome reality, it is not ultimately overpowering. Because of Jesus' resurrection, we also share in His resurrection, by trust. Death and resurrection are the true nature of Jesus' mission; humiliation and exaltation are in the proper order. The tragedy of Jesus' death is not a tragedy just because He died: it is a tragedy because our sins brought about His death. However, the tragedy becomes a triumph with His resurrection.

CHAPTER EIGHT

Difficult Teachings

Mark 9:33—10:52

Jesus Teaches Servanthood (9:33—10:31)

This section of teaching is in response to the learners' evident lack of understanding about the true nature of Jesus' mission. Jesus has just told them for the second time that He will be killed and rise after three days. Mark 9:32 states that the learners do not understand. Immediately after this, the learners argue about who is going to be the greatest in the kingdom, which indicates that they do not understand that Jesus just said He would be killed. The section begins with the argument among the learners, but it ends with Jesus' command to the learners to be at peace with one another (Mark 9:50). In between the argument and the command, Jesus teaches servanthood through a series of keyword pericopes. The keywords are *in the name, little ones, offends, fire,* and *salt.*

Receive the Kingdom Like a Child (33-37)

The question about who will be the greatest is common. I remember my frequent cry as a child, "I wanna be first." It is a human inclination, whether in a classroom, in contests, or at a stop sign. The learners, who are thinking of a kingdom on earth, argue who will go first behind Jesus. Perhaps the inner three, Peter, James, and John, were the prime combatants. When Jesus asks them concerning their argument, the learners at least know enough to remain silent. But Jesus will not let His opportunity fade, and He calls them together again to teach them.

Jesus' pronouncement is that if someone wants to be first, he or she must be last of all and servant to all. This is paralleled in Mark 8:34, where Jesus after the first prediction of His death tells the learners if someone wants to come after Him, that one must deny himself. Jesus is trying to teach the learners the meaning of following Him: it does not mean being the greatest or the first. On the contrary, it means being last, being a servant of all.

101

The learners' values are reversed. It is not a matter of prestige but of service. Jesus was first, but He became the servant of all. Paul makes this clear in Philippians 2:5-11, where Jesus, though equal to God, empties himself and takes the form of a slave. In Philippians 2:3, Paul encourages the Philippians to consider others better than themselves. A similar teaching appears in Romans 12:10, where Paul encourages the Roman Christians to outdo one another in showing honor.

We normally see people pushing others aside in order to be first. We rarely see people pushing others so they can be last or so they can help someone else, but that is exactly what Jesus is teaching here. Values are turned upside down, and the one who wants to be first must become a servant.

Jesus uses a nearby child to enact a parable for the learners. Whoever receives (accepts, welcomes) a child in the name of Jesus receives Jesus, and the one who receives Jesus actually receives God. The key word is *in the name.* There is also a play on words here because both the Aramaic and Greek words for child can also mean servant. The child here is a servant, but the child is a servant-believer, not an infant. We are all child-servants. None of us is better or greater than another.

The lesson for the learners and for us is that we should welcome one another as equal servants. If we do that, we really welcome Jesus, and if we welcome Jesus, we are really welcoming God. The clear lesson is that no one is greater; we ought to receive everyone equally. We are all equally servant-children, and as we receive each other, we receive God. Jesus' parable illustration of the child-servant is a direct rebuke to their seeking to be first. We should serve one another and not concern ourselves about who is going to be first.

Service in Christ's Name (38-41)

The keyword in the name occurs again in the next section, where John speaks on behalf of the Twelve. It is interesting to note that after each of the three predictions of Jesus' death, one (or two) of the inner three learners (Peter, John, and then James and John) contradicts Jesus' prediction, which shows they have misunderstand His mission.

John complains about a man who was throwing out demons in the name of Jesus. The learners had told the man to stop because the man was not following the Twelve. The argument about who is greatest has extended now beyond the Twelve to others, and the Twelve do not want others included. Recall that earlier, the learners had not been able to throw out a demon, and now they have stopped a man who is successful in throwing out demons in Jesus' name.

In Acts 19, some itinerant Jewish exorcists used Jesus' name to throw out demons and were taken over by the demons. The difference apparently lies in the trust in the name that this anonymous man had while the Jewish exorcists only used the name and did not trust in it. This anonymous man was successful because he worked in the name of Jesus.

Jesus tells John and the learners that they should not stop a person because he is able to do powerful things in Jesus' name. Such a person will not turn around and speak evil concerning Jesus, whose name he has been using.

The next statement by Jesus is radical because it is both inclusive and exclusive: "Whoever is not against us is for us" (Mark 9:40). His statement shows that there are two sides to the issue. This expression is inclusive because it includes many more than the Twelve or the ones currently following Jesus: it includes everyone not against Jesus. But there is no middle ground. If someone is against Jesus, then that person is excluded.

The saying about the cup of water also has the keyword phrase *in the name*. And this phrase is further explained by the expression *because you are of Christ* (Mark 9:41, A.T.). The way to welcome or accept or receive a follower of Christ is not to stop his good works, but to offer a cup of water—an especially significant gesture in an extremely dry land such as Palestine. To give a cup of water to a fellow believer is to give a cup of water to Jesus, and thus to God. Those who practice such welcoming hospitality will not lose their wage. A cup of water may seem trivial and certainly is the position of the servant who brings the water, but that is exactly the point. We are to serve one another and not stop one another; we are to serve in small ways with a cup, and in large ways by throwing out demons. No one is greater. We are all servants. Rather than forbidding, we should welcome and extend a cup of water.

If you do forbid or refuse the cup, you might cause offense to one of these little ones who believe in Him. The term *offense* has the sense of causing one of the believers to lose trust in Christ. The little ones who believe are not infants; they are the believers.

So Jesus is still on the subject of the relationships between followers: they are all His "little ones." The offense is serious and is indicated by the alternative. Jesus says it would be better if that person would have had a millstone tied around his neck and been thrown into the sea. The millstone mentioned here is not one for hand-grinding grain, but refers to a large millstone that is turned by a donkey.

Jesus' use of hyperbole drives home the point that one should not cause offense. Rather than causing offense, it would be better to welcome all believers. In welcoming believers, one welcomes Jesus and God. To offend believers is to offend Jesus and God. The point is that we all equally serve God and we ought to receive each other because we all work in the name of Christ.

What a lesson for today's church! Bickering, fighting, politics, and power plays too often are a part of the community of believers. These attitudes hinder the church in its major task of serving each other so everyone can reach out to those who have not yet accepted the name of Christ.

Priorities (9:42—10:31)

The keyword *offend* leads into the next section, which turns from causing offense to one's fellow believers to causing offense to himself. The three sayings about hand, foot, and eye are parallel. Rather than thinking in abstract terms, the Jew thought specifically of the part of the body that participated in the sin. This is only one of several indications that we should not take this section literally. The comparison is also parallel, except in reference to the eye; rather than "going into life," the parallel is "going into the kingdom of God." The use of hyperbole shows us how important our commitment must be to follow Jesus and not to give offense by our hands, feet, or eyes.

This is as radical as the saying concerning being for or against Christ. The opposite of life, or the kingdom of God, is "gehenna." *Gehenna* is an Aramaic word that refers to the valley of Hinnom, just outside Jerusalem. The Israelites had been condemned for sacrificing their children to the god Molech there (Jeremiah 7:31; 19:5; 32:35). Later, this valley served as a garbage dump that always burned. In late Judaism, *gehenna* became a term used to describe the place of divine punishment. The judgment of God on those who have rebelled against Him is described in Isaiah 66:24: there are corpses in which the worms never die and the fire is never quenched. Gehenna, the worm, and the fire are pictures of the judgment of God on those followers who cause offense to themselves by hand, foot, or eye. We must entirely eliminate, and without delay, whatever is in our lives that causes offense. There is no alternative except the fearful judgment of God.

The keyword *fire* is carried over from the previous section to the saying on "salt." "Everything will be salted in fire" (Mark 9:49, A.T.) is a reference to the persecution fires that Christians had to face in Rome. In the Old Testament, salt was added to the sacrifices. Christians believed their lives were living sacrifices to God, and, unfortunately, they sometimes became literal sacrifices. The Roman government's persecution tactics were well known by Mark's congregation since the reign of Nero. Christians lost their lives while covered in burning tar and pinned to crosses. It was a significant decision to follow Jesus in Mark's church.

The keyword *salt* is carried over from the previous saying, but the meaning of the word changes. Here salt is good. But if the salt becomes saltless, there is no way to regain its ability to season. It is this seasoning quality that is necessary for the relationships between the followers of Jesus. Paul tells the Christians in Colosse to let their speech always be with grace, seasoned with salt (Colossians 4:6). Salt gives flavor and also preserves. If salt loses its ability to flavor because of contaminants, it is worthless. For example, most of the salt from the Dead Sea area was worthless because the contaminants in it made its taste insipid and dull.

Jesus ends His teaching to His learners by telling them to have salt among themselves. They were to be a seasoning flavor to their fellow followers and to be at peace with one another. This admonition takes us back to the original setting for the teaching: the argument about who was greater. If we are going to argue at all, we should argue about who is last and who is servant of all. That would be an interesting argument!

Jesus leaves Jerusalem and goes to an area beyond the Jordan, but He continues teaching about servanthood. Mark comments that Jesus continues to teach, "as was his custom" (Mark 10:1). Mark quite often is not specific about the content of Jesus' teaching, but he is in this section. Chapter 10 begins with a transition from the concern for peace among the learners of Jesus and in the church to a concern for the peace between the individual learners and their families.

The discussion centers around divorce, children, and possessions, but the basic theme about the first being last and the last
being first continues, having begun at Mark 9:35. From there
through verse 50, the concern was with the inner workings of the
learners. Here the focus changes to the inner workings of the
learners' families (Mark 10:1-31). The issue is still servanthood
and how it is practiced.

The theme of common values reversal also continues. Divorce
is an acceptable practice, but Jesus teaches that it is not acceptable. Children are to be seen and not heard, but Jesus wants them
to come near. Possessions are thought to be a sign of God's blessings, but Jesus teaches that the learners may need to give away
what they think are God's blessings in order to enter the kingdom
of God. (Mark makes it clear that the teachings here are for the
learners of Jesus and those who would be His learners. Verse 10
indicates that Jesus is privately teaching His learners.) Jesus instructs the learners specifically that they are not to hinder children
(Mark 10:14). Jesus speaks to the learners directly about riches
and addresses them as children (Mark 10:24).

The situation concerning divorce is broached by the Pharisees,
who want to test Jesus by asking Him a legal question. They know
His answer will place Him in a predicament. They ask, "Is it
legal for a man to dismiss his wife?" (Mark 10:2, A.T.). A
debate concerning this question was prevalent in Jesus' time
between a liberal group of Jewish teachers led by Hillel (who
taught that a man could divorce his wife for almost any reason)
and a conservative group of Jewish teachers led by Shammai
(who taught that a man could divorce his wife only for sexual
misconduct.)

Jesus' answer to the question had both religious and political
interest. Mark has already mentioned that the Herodians, who
were a group favorable to Herod, were plotting with the Pharisees
to kill Jesus (Mark 3:6). Since this religious group was favorable
to Herod, the question about divorce was of great interest to
them. Herod had married a Nabatean princess for political purposes, but later decided to divorce her in order to marry Herodias,
the wife of Herod's half brother, Philip. Herodias left Philip, and
she and Herod were married. John the Baptist was beheaded as a
direct result of his condemning their marriage because Leviticus
18:16 and 20:21 teaches that it is illegal for a man to take his
brother's wife while his brother is still living.

Jesus' answer to the question of the legality of divorce is phrased as a question about what Moses really *commanded*. The Pharisees respond by saying that Moses *allowed* the writing of a certificate of divorce. The Scripture cited to justify this allowance is Deuteronomy 24:1. The Deuteronomy passage assumes the practice of divorce by a written certificate. It is in context a prohibition against a husband's remarrying a woman he has divorced after he has remarried and divorced again.

Divorce apparently is tolerated, but Jesus explains to the Pharisees that Moses wrote this command only because of the hardness of their heart. Divorce is allowed because of the sin in the world; it is there because of mankind's hard hearts, but faithfulness in marriage is approved by God. God condemns a husband's unfaithfulness and states clearly, "I hate divorce" (Malachi 2:13-16). Jesus points out to the Pharisees that although divorce is allowed by Moses, it is not God's intention.

Jesus tells the Pharisees the correct teaching of God. He refers to Genesis for the correct teaching concerning marriage: "From the beginning of creation God made them 'male and female' [Genesis 1:27]. For this reason a man shall leave his father and mother and be joined to his wife and the two will become one [Genesis 2:24]" (Mark 10:6-8, A.T.). Therefore, divorce is not a command; it is simply an allowance because of sin.

In the beginning, God created male and female, and they were created equally. It is interesting to note that it is the man who leaves his father and mother to be joined (literally glued to) his wife. Divorce is wrong because it separates the two who have become one flesh. Two people's becoming one is the mystery of marriage; it is what makes marriage. The bond is a bonding that God has performed; therefore, what God has yoked together, Jesus commands that a man should not separate. The reference to man is not to a judge in a law court, but to the husband of the woman who, in Jewish tradition, was the only one who could initiate a certificate of divorce.

We must be very careful in our teaching that we do not start to substitute our assumptions of what is right and wrong for the intention of God, which is clear in Scripture. This pertains not only to divorce, but to all issues.

The learners are concerned about what Jesus teaches since it goes against present values; so they ask Him more about it later when they are alone. Jesus replies with two statements that are entirely foreign to the Jewish mind of the first century: (1) "Anyone who divorces his wife and marries another woman commits adultery against her" (Mark 10:11). In Jewish custom, a man could never commit adultery against his wife, only against another man. (2) "And if she divorces her husband and marries another man, she commits adultery" (Mark 10:12). A Jewish woman could not initiate a divorce, although in Mark's Roman environment a woman could divorce her husband.

Thus Jesus reverses the current values of Jewish society again. A man who divorces (contrary to God's intention in creation) and remarries commits adultery against his first wife, and if a woman divorces (contrary to God's intention in creation and contrary to Jewish custom) and marries another, she also commits adultery.

There is no way through casuistry or rationalization that we can avoid Jesus' explicit teaching on this subject to His learners. It is a corrective teaching on the current lax view of divorce. One who divorces and marries again commits adultery. The adultery is against the first partner, not the new partner. Other texts teach us that the only exception is sexual immorality or if an unbelieving partner wishes the divorce. In the later case, Paul says that it is better to stay together if the unbeliever will stay. I think it is wrong also to assume that sexual immorality must lead to divorce. One who commits adultery within marriage or by remarriage can be forgiven. The only unforgivable sin is insulting the Holy Spirit, or actual unbelief.

The question of marriage leads to questions regarding children. Some adults had brought small children to Jesus for His blessing, following an ancient Jewish tradition that can be traced as far back as Genesis 48:14, when Israel (Jacob) blessed his sons. The learners, assuming that the children will bother Jesus, attempt to stop people from bringing their children. When Jesus sees the learners preventing children from coming to Him, He is angry. The word used here, translated "indignant," is a strong word and is another indication of Jesus' humanity.

When this particular word for anger is used in other Gospel contexts, it indicates an inappropriate anger. For example, the ten learners are angry when Peter and James want the best seats in the kingdom (Matthew 20:24; Mark 10:41). The learners are also angry at what they see as a waste of valuable ointment when a woman anoints Jesus (Matthew 26:8; Mark 14:4). The chief priests and the teachers of the law (Matthew 21:15), as well as a synagogue ruler (Luke 13:14), are also angry at Jesus. But all this is inappropriate anger. The only occurrence of this word as righteous anger is here in Mark 10:14.

Jesus was often unhappy with the Pharisees because they disapproved of His doing good, especially on the Sabbath, or His associating with tax collectors and sinners. Here, Jesus is upset in the same way with His learners. They do not understand that Jesus came especially for these kinds of people. Jesus is a special advocate for the sick, the demon-possessed, the deaf, the sinners, the women and children, and all the other people who are virtually ignored by the Pharisees and Jewish leaders.

Jesus says, "Let the little children come to me" (Mark 10:14). Jesus is the kingdom; so the children should be allowed to come. "Do not hinder them," He says, using the same prohibition He used earlier when the learners had made a mistake about the exorcist who was throwing out demons in the name of Jesus but was not traveling with the learners and Jesus. Jesus told the learners not to "hinder" him.

Jesus explains the last statement concerning the kingdom of God (that the kingdom "belongs to such as these") by saying that a person must receive the kingdom as a small child in order to enter. The small child here is most likely an allusion to the child's status, not to any merit the child might have. It is the children's status that makes the learners reject them. Merit is not what enables a child to enter into the kingdom: it is because a child is weak and powerless in society. It is this weak and powerless status that enables children to accept or receive the kingdom. Children accept gifts with no questions; adults wonder why the gifts are given. We must be like children and acknowledge our powerlessness in order to receive the power of God to become the children of God.

Jesus holds the children in His arms, puts His hands on them, and blesses them. This is a beautiful picture of Jesus' humanity, and is probably written to provide a deliberate contrast to His anger that is depicted in verse 14. Both are human emotions, and both are appropriate at the right times. Jesus can be the tender shepherd who gathers the sheep, but He is also the shepherd who separates the sheep from the goats.

In addition to discussing the subjects of divorce and children, Jesus discusses the attitudes of His learners about their possessions. The incident about a good and wealthy man provides the impetus for this private discussion. A man runs up to Jesus, kneels before Him, and questions Jesus. In the running, kneeling, and questioning words, Mark not only shows action but also demonstrates the man's urgency (since he runs), the respect the man has for Jesus (since he kneels), and his inquiring mind (since he questions Jesus).

The man also addresses Jesus with a term of respect that Judaism did not allow. The term *good* was almost exclusively reserved for references to God. So Jesus first corrects the man in terms of his address of Jesus as "Good Teacher." While not denying the man's description, Jesus wonders what the man thinks of the term. Jesus replies that no one is good except God. Does the man really imply that Jesus is God? The man addresses Jesus as teacher and leaves out the word *good* later (Mark 10:20); so Jesus makes His point by directing the man to God and not to himself. This is the point of Jesus' comment: "You know the commands"—that is, the commands of God (Mark 10:19, A.T.).

The man's question is simple and straightforward: "What must I do to inherit eternal life?" (Mark 10:17). Life was always sought by the Jew, and God promised life to those who repented from sin and practiced justice and rightness (Deuteronomy 30:15-20; Ezekiel 33:15, 16). This life was viewed not as simply life here on earth, but a life in the age to come. (Age-to-come life was perceived as still an earthly life, but it was life in a wholly God-ruled state with all physical pleasures involved. It was not what Christians call eternal life.) We learn later that this man who came to Jesus was wealthy. He was living well and already had a good life, but he was seeking life in the coming age. The man probably thought he was close to his goal, but he came to Jesus, a recognized teacher, for more assurance.

The commands that Jesus gives are the fifth through the ninth of the Ten Commandments given to Moses on Mt. Sinai. The first four, which relate to an individual's relationship to God, are omitted. The commands to have no other gods, no idols, not to take the name of God in vain, and to remember the Sabbath are a given way of life for Jews. They indicate the uniqueness of Judaism. The later six commands were known and practiced by many civilizations, but the first four laws were not.

The command not to defraud is peculiar in this setting because it is not one of the Ten. Some scholars believe that this command is a restatement of commands eight and nine (prohibiting stealing

110

and lying) since to *defraud* means to steal by lying. Others see this command not to defraud as a restatement of the tenth command against greediness.

The man's reply to Jesus' initial answer is that he has guarded all these commands from the time he took upon himself the obligations of the law (probably at age thirteen). It seems presumptuous to us for anyone to claim to have perfectly kept the commands. However, this was not unusual for a religious Jew then, especially a Pharisee. Followers of Judaism considered it possible to keep these ten commands without breaking any of them.

Mark shows us a very sincere and anxious man who questions Jesus with respect. He is seeking a noble cause because he wants life in the age to come. He is a practicing Jew, but he feels (correctly) that he still lacks something. Normally, keeping the law would be enough, but this man is perceptive enough to realize that there is more than the law.

Jesus notes that the man is sincere and, looking at him, loves him. Here is an ideal convert: one who is asking for salvation. But although Jesus loves him, His love is also able to confront the man about his lack. Jesus tells him that he lacks one thing, and then gives him five commands:

Go!

Sell as much as you have!

Give to the poor and you will have treasure in Heaven!

Come.

Follow Me.

The wealthy and good Jew would already have given to the poor. This was one of three deeds of rightness that many Jews practiced. But Jesus tells him to sell all his possessions and give the proceeds to the poor. The one thing the man lacks is trust in God. Jesus touches the heart of this person's priorities. His ultimate priority is not God, but his wealth. He trusts in that.

Life obviously cannot be purchased, and Jesus does not imply that a person can purchase life by selling all he or she owns. Life is given as a gift from God to those who desire it. This man did not want it badly enough. New life involves not only deeds, but a change of life, of commitment, and of priorities. This new demand lets go of human security and lets God supply all that is needed. The *go, sell,* and *give* were only preludes to Jesus' full answer to the rich man's question. The complete answer is to *come* and *follow* Jesus, because this is the way to have life.

The man left, sad and grieving at Jesus' invitation. This is the only recorded refusal Jesus ever has to His challenge for a person to follow Him. The reason for the refusal is that the man has many possessions and cannot let them go. The man does not argue with Jesus, but he leaves filled with gloom and sorrow.

After this episode, Jesus tells His learners privately that it is difficult for a wealthy person to enter the kingdom of God. The issue here is riches and entering the kingdom. The problem is that the rich often trust in their wealth and not in God. The rich think they can do something to enter the kingdom, perhaps even purchase their entrance. The rich are not like children who receive gifts openly and willingly.

The learners of Jesus recognize that Jesus teaches yet another reversal of Jewish thought. Material possessions are a sign of blessings from God for Jews. This attitude is pictured in Job 1:10 and 42:10: Satan says that Job has been blessed by God in all his wealth. Job loses his wealth but in the end—because of his rightness—he gains back not just what he lost but two times what he originally had. If it is true that riches are a sign of the blessings of God, and if it is equally true that it is hard for a rich person to enter into the kingdom, it is no wonder that the learners are amazed.

Jesus makes a more general statement about the difficulty of entering the kingdom because He knows that His learners still do not understand. Jesus illustrates His point by hyperbole. In a hyperbole, words are taken literally so the point of the discussion cannot be missed. Jesus says that there is no way that a camel can go through the eye of a needle! Attempts to identify a gate in the wall of Jerusalem as a "needle gate" were popular among Christians in medieval times but are incorrect. It is also incorrect to say that the word for *camel* was misspelled and should be translated "rope." The fact is that a very large animal cannot go through a very small hole! The learners finally understand the point.

The astonished learners ask who is able to be saved. They realize that from Jesus' illustration, no one can save himself, especially if the rich who are blessed by God because of their goodness are not able to enter the kingdom, then others not blessed by God would have still less chance. There is an interesting series of parallel expressions in this account. The man asks about inheriting eternal life, and Jesus talks about entering the kingdom of God. The learners respond by asking who is able to be saved. *Salvation, eternal life,* and entrance into the *kingdom of God* are simply three analogies for the same idea.

The point of the hyperbole is that it is impossible for anyone to be saved. Jesus repeats this point when He says with men, it is not possible. But what is not possible with men is possible with God! It is not possible to gain the kingdom by attainments or by the selling of possessions; the kingdom is not automatically yours if you are rich or poor; it is not automatically yours if you obey all the rules (Ten Commandments). The kingdom is God's gift to all people, but it must be accepted. It is not true that the rich man could not enter the kingdom; he simply did not accept the gift of Jesus' invitation. Even if the rich man had sold all that he owned and given the proceeds to the poor, he still had to follow in trust. To gain the kingdom requires trust in God: not in riches, or poverty, or position, or humility, and not in self. We must trust God, who makes possible the impossible—that is, that sinners can become saints.

Peter hears all that Jesus teaches and comments that he and the other learners have left everything behind to follow Jesus. There is an implication here that Peter feels they have a right to the kingdom. Jesus denies this because anyone who has left house, brothers, sisters, mother, father, children, or fields will receive all of these things again.

The person who has left any of these things must have left them because of Jesus and the good message He teaches. Note that if a person has left a house on account of Jesus, that person will receive back not simply houses, but all the rest as well. In other words, a person not only receives back what he or she loses, but one hundred times what is lost, plus all the other things as well. The things are received now in this age, but with persecutions. The hundred times arises from the fact that the servants of Jesus, as they go about their service, gain access to many houses in the Christian community, they gain hundreds of brothers, sisters, mothers, and children, and they gain benefits from many fields. Ministers can testify to having access to many homes, to well-spread tables, and to people who treat them as family members.

But Jesus says His learners will have other consequences. Persecution followed Jesus and His learners. Persecution followed Paul and the early church. The learners do not have a right to the kingdom because they have left all to follow Jesus. They will receive back one hundred times what they leave behind, but with persecutions. We do not receive the benefit of trusting Jesus immediately. The real benefit comes in the next age because it is eternal life.

The receipt of eternal life is not the result of leaving all and following Jesus, either for the rich man who rejects the invitation or for the learners who leave all and follow Jesus. Eternal life is the result of trust in Jesus; it is not a reward. It is so superior, and so surpasses any act or deed, that to speak of it as "reward" is ridiculous: it is too far out of proportion to the work. The rich man, interested in material values, does not realize the eternal value he has turned down. Peter thinks that leaving all and following Jesus is a guarantee of a place in the kingdom.

Jesus concludes His teaching with an expression similar to what He used at the beginning of this section: "Many who are first will be last, and the last first" (Mark 10:31). We have come full circle to the first description of what it means to be a follower: it means to be last, to be the servant of all.

We have yet to learn that lesson well.

The Third Prediction of Jesus' Death (10:32-34)

Jesus and His followers are on the road to Jerusalem. The learners know that the road to Jerusalem is a road to certain death. The followers are amazed at Jesus' directness and are afraid of the prospect of death; yet they follow. They do not understand everything about Jesus and are slow in their trust, but they still follow Him. In the third explanation of His death and resurrection, Jesus takes the learners aside to explain what will occur. Jesus says clearly, "We are going up to Jerusalem" (Mark 10:33). When Jesus announces this in the Gospel according to John, the learners know that the Jews are planning to stone Him, and Thomas speaks out for the learners, "Let us also go, that we may die with him" (John 11:7-16).

This prediction is very similar to the other two, except there are more details. The Son of Man is first given over to the chief priests and scribes, who condemn Him to death. These Jews then give Jesus over to the Gentiles. There is tremendous irony in the Jews' handing their Messiah over to the Gentiles for execution. The Gentiles then mock Him, spit at Him, scourge Him, and finally execute Him.

In these predictions, Jesus sees himself as the suffering servant mentioned in Isaiah 52 and 53 and Psalm 22:6-8. Mark faithfully reproduces these nuances because he wants his church to understand that the real nature of Jesus' service was not earthly kingship and power, and so these things should not interest the Christian.

What appears extraordinary to the reader of Mark is that the prediction of Jesus' tragic death is really overcome by the prediction of His rising again after three days. The learners hear all that Jesus says, and they are afraid because He speaks of persecution and death, but they miss the last point concerning what will happen after three days. An essential ingredient of the good message occurs "after three days." There is no good news if we stop at Jesus' betrayal and death, even His vicarious death for us. The good news must include the announcement that after three days, *He arose!*

The content of Jesus' prediction is the content of the good message for Mark's church and for us. It is the death and resurrection of Jesus. This is good news because He gave His life as a ransom in the place of many (Mark 10:45). The "many" includes us and any others to whom we tell the good message. The good message includes the forgiveness of our sins and life after death because He died and was raised from the dead after three days.

Jesus Again Teaches Servanthood (10:35-45)

To James and John (35-40)

Again Mark shows clearly that the learners do not understand that the real nature of Jesus' Christhood was suffering service, fulfilled in the humiliation of death by crucifixion. Immediately after Jesus talks about the true nature of His service, two leaders of the learners ask for the chief places of honor in what they think will be Jesus' new earthly kingdom. This incident with James and John is framed by the contrasting servanthood of Jesus in Mark 10:33 and 34 and Mark 10:45.

James and John address Jesus as Teacher and, unbelievably, ask Jesus to give them whatever they ask! This is an all-inclusive request that Jesus does not grant. Jesus asks them specifically what they want Him to do. Jesus wants the two to be explicit; perhaps Jesus wants them to hear their own words of ambition. James and John are not reticent; they ask Jesus for the two best seats of honor when Jesus comes in His glory. They understand glory as the coming of the great kingdom where all the enemies of

God will be destroyed and a great peace will reign over all the earth, with Jesus as king. They want to be seated next to the king.

Jesus understands glory as the crucifixion and resurrection. It is interesting to note that thieves were on the right and left of Jesus when He was in glory on the cross. Since the glory of Jesus is the cross, it is certainly true that James and John do not know what they are asking—and Jesus tells them that in no uncertain terms.

The next two references are a continuation of Jesus' identification of himself as the suffering servant. Jesus asks James and John whether they are able to drink the cup that He drinks or be immersed in the immersion in which He is about to be immersed. Their glib answer indicates that they still do not know what they are saying. Although the cup in the Old Testament means both a cup of joy (Psalm 23:5) and sorrow (Isaiah 51:17, 22), it is clear that Jesus alludes to the same cup that He refers to in Mark 14:36, which is the cup of suffering and sorrow. Jesus must drink this cup as He suffers and dies on our behalf.

The reference to *immersion* is a parallelism to *cup,* and simply means that Jesus will soon be immersed in suffering. Jesus' surprising reply to their glib answer, "We are able," is that they will indeed drink such a cup and be immersed in such an immersion. Tradition tells us that all the apostles except John died as martyrs. This is also a fulfillment of Jesus' earlier reply that the followers will have one hundred times houses, fields, and such—but with persecution.

To the Other Learners (41-45)

In telling James and John that the places to the left and right of the King are not His to give, Jesus does not correct their false understanding of an earthly kingdom. The other ten learners are upset when they learn about James and John's request. They probably had similar pretension for the chief positions in the coming kingdom, and this might well be their reason for being upset.

Jesus summons all the learners together to explain the nature of true service again. It was as true then as it is now that those who "think" they rule their nations love to exercise total control and to "lord it over" others (Mark 10:42). This is the way of the world. This is how we are taught from infancy. The concept of servanthood is repugnant to most people. The concepts of power, authority, prestige, and honor go together and do not generally include servanthood. Note that Jesus says that those who "think" they rule fool themselves. Actually, God is the ultimate Ruler, and all authority comes from Him: rulers only appear to rule as they attempt to exercise total control and "lord it over" others.

The learners of Jesus should realize they are followers, and they should follow His example. The desire to be great can be filled by being a servant in the kingdom. The desire to be first can be filled by being slave of all. While we recoil at the idea of being a servant, we find the idea of becoming a slave even more repugnant. Jesus is reversing human values again. Jesus has taught His servant concept before, but His followers have not learned it yet; so He must repeat His teaching. (One aspect of servanthood is the repetitive nature of many tasks.) Ultimately, Jesus demonstrates His greatness by being a servant and how He is first by being a slave when He yields to death on the cross.

If anyone deserves to have been served, it should have been God's Son. But the One who should have been served came to serve and give His life as a ransom. The word *ransom* refers to deliverance or redemption by purchase. War prisoners were released by the payment of a certain price in Biblical times. *Ransom* was also the term used for the process in which a slave was released. The slave brought the price of his freedom to the temple, gave it to the god, and was released. (In reality, the temple keeper gave the slave's price to his owner.)

The idea of redemption is part of the suffering-servant concept that Jesus' life illustrates. In Isaiah 53:10, there is a reference to the suffering servant who gives himself as a guilt offering. The guilt offering discussion in Leviticus 5, 6, and 7 describes the atonement process for various sins; the sinner brings a live animal that is sacrificed for the sins of the person. Jesus becomes our guilt offering and is killed for our sins.

Jesus is the supreme example of reversed values. The Son of God serves and gives His life. Since that is true, the followers of the Son of God must live their lives in the same manner. Jesus wants His followers to understand the servant-nature of the kingdom. Mark wants his church to understand that following Jesus means serving. We have yet to learn the true servant attitude.

The Healing of Blind Bartimaeus (10:46-52)

Jesus' healing of the blind beggar Bartimaeus is the last healing miracle that Mark relates before beginning his book's conclusion with the triumphal entry into Jerusalem. The Bartimaeus story repeats two of Mark's major themes: the power of Jesus in healing and that Jesus is acknowledged as the Messiah (by the appellation "Son of David"). The outcast, in this case a blind man, is treated well, receives a blessing, understands who Jesus is, and follows Jesus as a learner. Mark shows that it is the unacknowledged people who understand Jesus and accept Him. This story is an appropriate conclusion to the earlier three-prediction section in which Jesus explains the true nature of His servanthood. Not everyone is as "dull" as the close learners of Jesus. In this incident, a blind man has the trust to "see" Jesus as the "Son of David," Healer, Master Teacher, and One worthy of being followed. The idea of the blind's seeing more than those who have no impairment is further emphasized because the three-prediction section begins and ends with Jesus' healing the blind (Mark 8:22-26 and 10:46-52).

Jericho is about eighteen miles northeast of Jerusalem. The road to Jerusalem in Jesus' time was a slow hilly climb, frequently traveled but known to be dangerous. The blind beggar is sitting along the road outside Jericho. He has heard that Jesus is coming and begins to shout, "Son of David, have mercy on me!" (Mark 10:47). The shout indicates not only that he is blind but that he has heard about the power of Jesus. The words *Son of David* have messianic overtones according to Isaiah 11:1 and Jeremiah 23:5 and 6. The cry of the beggar is a cry of David in the Psalms (Psalms 4:1; 6:2; 41:4).

The crowd rebukes the beggar, but he continues to shout in order to catch Jesus' attention. The crowd rebukes him not for saying, "Son of David," but because he is a nuisance. It appears that "streetpeople" were not appreciated any more in Jesus' time than they are now. Jesus (for the third time in this section on His true nature) does not allow the rebuke, just as He did not allow Peter's rebuke (Mark 8:32), or the learners' rebuke of the children (Mark 10:13). Jesus calls for the man to come. Jesus has always sought out the insignificant persons who are ignored.

There are several indications that this is an eyewitness account: the crowd relays the message of Jesus and now encourages the man rather than rebuking him; and the man throws off his outer coat, leaps up (a word unique in the New Testament), and comes to Jesus. These small details demonstrate what many feel are details given to Mark by Peter, who was an eyewitness.

Jesus' conversation with the man is brief. Jesus asks him what he wants, probably to allow the man to express his trust. The man asks for his eyesight to be restored. Mark mentions no particular action by Jesus except His words, "Go, your trust has brought sight to your eyes" (Mark 10:52, A.T.). Mark closes the section by saying that the man has his vision returned immediately, and he follows Jesus. Up to this point, Jesus did not want those He healed to follow Him. But this man follows Jesus because he trusts and because he stands in contrast to the other followers who do not see clearly, but still follow Jesus.

This section shows that Jesus is a servant and that He calls others to be servants. The emphasis on humility and service are illustrated by Jesus' service to the lowly rather than the mighty; the sick, not the healthy; the sinner, not the self-righteous. The section is a powerful call to Mark's church and to us to abandon smugness and exclusiveness and cry with the blind man, "Son of David, have mercy on us."

Part Three

Jesus Demonstrates the True Nature and Purpose of His Sonship

Mark 11:1—16:20

CHAPTER NINE

Triumphal Entry

Mark 11:1-26

The third section of Mark moves from the teaching of Jesus to the actual demonstration of the true nature of His Sonship, especially in His death, burial, and resurrection.

Jesus comes into the court of those who want Him killed. Aware of their intentions, Jesus shows through a series of teachings and actions that the way of Messiahship is the way of betrayal, death, and resurrection.

The Messianic Entrance Into Jerusalem (11:1-11)

When Jesus plans an entrance into Jerusalem on a colt, He demonstrates His knowledge of His identity and purpose. Jesus sends two of His learners to a village to bring back a colt for His transportation into Jerusalem. His instructions are precise: they are to go to a particular village and immediately as they enter they will find a colt tied, on which no one has sat. They are to untie the colt and bring it to Jesus. If anyone asks what they are doing, they are to reply that the lord (probably meaning owner) has need of it and will send the colt back immediately. The learners go into the village and find the colt tied at an outside door on the street. As they untie the colt, some people who see them ask why they are untying the colt. The learners reply as Jesus instructed and bring the colt back to Jesus (Mark 11:1-6).

These actions by Jesus are a direct fulfillment of the prophecy in Zechariah 9:9:

> Rejoice greatly, O Daughter of Zion!
>   Shout, Daughter of Jerusalem!
> See, your king comes to you,
>   righteous and having salvation,
> gentle and riding on a donkey,
> on a colt, the foal of a donkey.

The fact that the colt has never been used before is appropriate because in the Old Testament, animals used for sacred purposes were not to have been used previously (cf. Deuteronomy 21:3).

While Jesus is cognizant of His Messiahship in these actions, it is not apparent that the crowds are. The learners spread their outer clothing on the colt and on the path. They and the crowds spread branches of trees along the way. Both those in front of Jesus and those behind Him sing, "Hosanna! Blessed is he who comes in the name of the Lord!" (Mark 11:9). The song is the Hallel from Psalm 118:24 and 25. The crowds around Jesus at this time are other Jewish pilgrims who have come from some distance to the Passover festival.

The high point to such a pilgrimage was a climb to the top of the Mount of Olives where a dramatic view of the entire city of Jerusalem with its majestic temple was suddenly visible below. The happy, exalting pilgrims honor Jesus as they descend into the city of Jerusalem. The crowds here honor Jesus not as Messiah, but as a well-known teacher and healer. The Psalm is the normal song sung at both the Festival of the Tabernacles and the Passover. The expression *blessed is the one coming in the name of the Lord* (A.T.) is a reference to any pilgrim who comes to the holy city. Verse 11 mentions no crowds, and is rather anticlimactic if Jesus had been recognized as the Messiah who would deliver the Jews from Roman bondage. It is made explicit in John 12:16 that the learners did not understand this manner of entry until after Jesus' death, burial, and resurrection.

Jesus is aware of His Messiahship and so is Mark. This song sung by the pilgrims is especially appropriate for Mark because Psalm 118 is about a man rejected at first (118:7, 22), who is recognized as righteous (118:14, 15), and who enters the city (118:19) to shouts of praise (118:25, 26). Psalm 118:22 refers to the stone the builders rejected as having become the chief cornerstone. This is especially important because it is used later by several New Testament authors to identify Jesus. The second half of the song sung at Jesus' entrance is not from the Psalm, but is a chiastic response to the first stanza: it repeats the content of the first stanza, but in reverse.

After the descent to Jerusalem, with its spontaneous and joyful celebration, Jesus goes into the city and to the temple. Jesus takes time to look around, but, because it is late, He returns to Bethany to spend the night.

The Fig Tree (11:12-14)

In the morning, on the way from Bethany to Jerusalem, Jesus is hungry and notices a fig tree in the distance and goes to pick some fruit. This incident is told in two parts with the story of the cleaning of the temple in between. The temple-cleaning event between the two parts of the fig tree story is interpreted by it, and the fig tree story is clarified by the temple-cleaning story. The temple, which is supposed to be a house of prayer, will be destroyed just as the fig tree with green leaves, supposed to be producing figs, was withered by Jesus' curse.

This particular fig tree leafs out in the spring after the fruit has set. The fruit, however, does not ripen until the summer. When Jesus comes to the tree, He finds only leaves. The fruit has not set. (Mark comments that it was not the season for figs—Mark 11:13). The point is not that Jesus expects to eat, although hunger drew His attention initially to the tree. This tree with green leaves promises fruit but does not even have figs developing. This is an allusion to Micah 7, where Micah speaks for God in saying that there is not a cluster of grapes to eat nor a first-ripe fig, and this is analogous to the fact that the godly person has disappeared from the land and there is no righteous person among the people. All of this draws attention to the temple, which is not producing righteous people and therefore will be destroyed.

> I will take away their harvest, declares the Lord.
>> There will be no grapes on the vine.
> There will be no figs on the tree,
>> and their leaves will wither.
> What I have given them
>> will be taken from them (Jeremiah 8:13).

Because there is no promise of figs, Jesus says that no one will ever eat from this tree. Peter understands that Jesus pronounces a curse on the tree (Mark 11:21). Isaiah 34:4 mentions the withering of a vine or fig tree as the judgment and destruction of God against the nations.

This incident is a type of prophetic sign or symbolic action on Jesus' part to show God's wrath against the temple and Jerusalem. In Isaiah 20:1-6, Isaiah walked naked and shoeless as a sign and token against Egypt and a prediction that the King of Assyria would take the young of Egypt captive both naked and barefoot.

The prophetic action by Jesus is not understood by the learners, but is clarified to the readers through the next event, which is the cleaning of the temple.

Cleaning the Temple (11:15-19)

It was necessary to have animals available for sacrifices in the temple so that those who came to Jerusalem from long distances could purchase animals for sacrifice. Oxen were sold for the wealthy, while pigeons were made available to those of lesser means. It was also necessary for money changers to be present because the temple tax had to be paid in Jewish coinage. Individuals from other countries had to exchange their money in order to pay their tax. Thus, Jesus' action was not simply against buying and selling, but against the charging of extremely high prices and against the confusion the buying and selling caused in the temple supposedly devoted to the worship of God. The exchanging process occurred in the courtyard of the Gentiles. If an inquiring Gentile had come to the temple to learn more about the Jewish God, he would have walked into the equivalent of a bustling bazaar—full of noise and confusion.

Jesus quotes from Isaiah 56:7 that the house of God (the temple) would be called a house of prayer for all nations. This was the purpose of the temple, especially for the Gentiles who were only allowed into this particular courtyard. But the temple rulers had made the house of prayer a cave of robbers.

This drastic action by Jesus brings two opposite reactions. The temple rulers, chief priests, and scribes hear what Jesus says and decide that Jesus must be destroyed. Their decision comes not simply because of what He says, but because the crowds like what He says and are astonished at what He teaches. The reaction of the crowds is astonishment, probably at Jesus' drastic action, but probably also because they agree with Him concerning the confusion and the dealers' exorbitant prices.

The Fig Tree and Prayer (11:20-26)

After cursing the fig tree and cleaning the temple of "robbers," Jesus leaves the city that evening for Bethany. It is twenty-four hours after Jesus cursed the tree when He and His learners are on their way back to Jerusalem, pass the fig tree, and find that it has dried up from the roots. Being dried up "from the roots" means that this tree will never again be able to produce fruit. Peter remembers the earlier event and exclaims to Jesus that the tree Jesus cursed is dried up.

As the fig tree's barrenness anticipated the temple cleaning, the temple—which was to be a house of prayer—anticipates this section on trust and prayer. Jesus answers Peter's exclamation with the encouragement to trust in God (Mark 11:22). This alludes to the fact that Jesus trusted and the fig tree dried up. It is implied that the learners need to trust in God for the future condemnation of Jerusalem and for the future blessings that they will receive. Trust is the real point to this section and is mentioned several times.

The reference to "this mountain" (Mark 11:23) is probably a reference to the Mount of Olives, on which they were standing. The Dead Sea can be seen from this location. The example of a prayer request is a hyperbole, that is, an exaggeration to emphasize a point. The point is not to be able to throw hills into the sea, but that one must trust in order to have prayers answered. A person cannot doubt and still ask in trust.

The concept of trust is repeated in the next verse, which says that as much as we pray and ask, we must trust. In fact, we must trust as though we have already received that for which we have prayed.

While still on the topic of prayer, Jesus includes the saying about forgiveness as an essential to answered prayer. This indicates that prayer is not simply asking for things. Prayer does not consist only of our relationship to God, but also of our relationship with others. We cannot be out of relationship with fellow Christians and be in relationship with God. Our forgiveness of others occurs in our prayers because we need God's help for us to be able to forgive others. If we are unable to forgive others in our prayers, we cannot expect God to answer our prayers for the forgiveness of our own sins.

The cleaning of the house of prayer and Jesus' ability to curse a fig tree gives Jesus an occasion to teach His learners the essentials of prayer. Trust is mentioned three times and its corollary, not to doubt, once. To ask and to be forgiving are the other two important elements mentioned in this text.

CHAPTER TEN

Demanding Questions

Mark 11:27—12:44

The Question of Authority (11:27-33)

Jesus is in Jerusalem again and teaches in the temple, which is the focal point for the last week of His earthly service. The chief priests, scribes, and elders come to Him. The three groups are mentioned together five times in Mark, and in every case they are the Sanhedrin, which is the supreme council for Jews. The Sanhedrin has both legislative and judicial power. We presume that those who come to Jesus represent the whole group.

The men come to Jesus to ask Him by what authority He does the things He does. They ask Him whether He claims to be a prophet from God, or perhaps they use vague words to see whether He might claim to be the Messiah. The authoritative word of cleaning the temple and the authoritative teaching that He has given must have some validity in the mind of those who question Him. Perhaps they seek additional accusations against Him. The second version of their question asks who gave Him the authority to teach and to clean the temple. This is a legitimate question asked by legitimate authorities who have the task of regulating temple activities.

In typical rabbinic style, Jesus says that He will ask them one question, and if they answer, He will then answer their question. Jesus' question is also about authority. Jesus inquires what they think about the authority of John the Baptist. This is phrased in a question about the immersion of John, and whether it was from Heaven or from men (Mark 11:30), but the question about immersion is a reference to the whole service of John, of which immersion was the significant action. The alternatives of "from Heaven" (really a paraphrastic expression for God) or "from men" severely limits the ability of Jesus' opponents to answer. Jesus wants them to answer His question, however, because He says, "Answer me," in His initial statement (Mark 11:29) and again, "Tell me," at the end of His question (Mark 11:30). Jesus does not ask His question in order to evade their question to Him.

With only two alternatives, the representatives from the Sanhedrin debate how they should answer. The implication of saying that the immersion is from God is that John's authority is from God, and if John's authority is from God, then why did the Jewish leaders not trust John? The implication of saying that John's immersion is simply a man's idea is not stated openly by the debaters, but it is clear from Mark's comments. The leaders fear the crowds, who believe that John was a prophet with authority from God to preach and immerse.

The leaders choose a third alternative and pretend ignorance. They cannot or dare not admit the work of God by John, but they do not want to inflame the crowd by denying John's authority. Note that the leaders who are supposed to legitimize teaching will not say what is legitimate. Another implication of their feigned ignorance is that they have rejected John, who is from God, and they will reject Jesus. If they had accepted John, they would have had to accept Jesus. John pointed the way to Jesus, who had equal favor with the people. Jesus had just received a favorable reception by people at His entrance into Jerusalem and after He cleaned the temple.

Jesus then refuses to tell the representatives by what authority He acts. Jesus knows His authority but refuses to say. However, Jesus does tell them in the following parallel story what His authority is, and the leaders understand part of the story.

The Vineyard Parallel Story (12:1-12)

The story about the vineyard is a continuation of the question about authority and is really a question about the rejection of authority and Jesus. The parable is not a prediction or an allegory, but it is a warning parable because it warns the representatives of the Sanhedrin against what they are planning to do to Jesus. The description of the vineyard closely follows the parable in Isaiah 5, where God plants a vineyard, sets a hedge around it, builds a tower, and digs a winepress. The critical difference is that in Isaiah, it is the vineyard itself (i.e., all Israel) that produces worthless grapes while in Jesus' parable, it is the farmers (Jewish leaders) who are at fault and not the vineyard.

In Jesus' parable, the vineyard is leased to tenant farmers by an absentee landlord. (The circumstances are common enough to country life in Galilee: absentee landlords are abundant.) When the time comes for the landlord to receive some of the crops of the land, he sends a servant to collect. The servant is beaten and sent away empty-handed. Other servants are sent, and they also are beaten, wounded, dishonored, or killed. (Unfortunately, rebellion by tenant farmers is also well known in the Galilean area.)

Finally, the father sends his loved son. The expression *loved son* (Mark 12:6) means his only son. When the tenant farmers see the son coming, they presume the father is dead and the son is coming to collect his inheritance. They reason that if they kill the son, they will be able to keep the land; so they kill him and throw his body outside the vineyard.

Jesus asks what recourse the owner has. It is not often that Jesus answers His own question, but He does in this case. He wants to issue a warning in the strongest possible way. He notes that the owner will destroy the tenant farmers and give the vineyard to others. The implication is that if the Jewish leaders kill Jesus as they are planning, God will also bring about their destruction.

The quotation of Psalm 118:22, 23 about the stone the builders rejected (Mark 12:10, 11) is from the same Psalm the people sang when Jesus entered Jerusalem. It is the Hallel, which is sung at the Passover. Jesus uses this quotation to interpret the parable in order to point to His Messiahship. This is Peter's interpretation when he preaches (in Acts 4:11) and again in his first letter (1 Peter 2:7). Mark's church also understands this as a declaration of Jesus' messiahship. But the Jewish leaders understand the parable to mean that they are about to reject another of God's messengers. Mark makes it clear that Jesus is not simply another of God's messengers, but God's loved Son. There are serious consequences for such a rejection: the first consequence is their personal destruction, and the second consequence is the loss of the vineyard to others (the destruction of Israel).

When the representatives of the Sanhedrin realize what Jesus is saying, they try to seize Him. They are unable to do so, however, because of the crowd, who has accepted Jesus as having authority. The leaders leave to report their experience and to continue to lay plans to capture Jesus.

The Question About Taxes (12:13-17)

Having been frustrated in its attempt to bring about Jesus' arrest, the Sanhedrin sends a formal delegation of Pharisees and

Herodians to "trap" Jesus in His own words. The Herodians and Pharisees form a curious combination—they do not normally associate with each other. The Herodians are a political party that supports Herod, and the Pharisees, while comfortable with the government, do not favor Herod. The word *trap* is used only once in the New Testament, but it is used in the classical Greek language as a reference to the hunting of animals.

The delegation tries to trap Jesus by flattering Him so that He will feel obligated to answer their trick question. They address Him as teacher; they say that He always tells the truth; they say that He is impartial in all matters because He does not look at the person and make decisions on the basis of who is questioning; they say that He really teaches the way of God in truth. The delegation is obviously not sincere in their compliments: the narrative says earlier that they are trying to trap Him and later notes that Jesus understands their hypocrisy. The five characteristics that the Sanhedrin use in their trick questions are true attributes of Jesus; so the opponents of Jesus proclaim His rightness in spite of their hypocrisy.

The trick question concerns whether it is correct for a Jew to give the head tax to Caesar or not. The head tax was based on a census, and all Jews had to pay their tax in Roman coin. The question is repeated: "Shall we give or can we not give?" The delegation thinks it has Jesus in a quandary. If Jesus says to give, He will acknowledge Roman rule over Israel. The problem for some Jews was that the coin they had to use to pay taxes had the image of Caesar Augustus and gave him divine honors. If Jesus says not to give, then the Roman government surely has cause to retaliate against Him.

Jesus asks the delegation why they are attempting to trick Him. Jesus is aware of their hypocrisy; so He tells them to show Him a denarius. (The denarius is a common silver coin equal to a worker's daily wage. The coin has Caesar's head on one side with the inscription, "Tiberias Caesar Augustus son of the Divine Augustus." The opposite side has a seated image of his mother, Livia, with the inscription, "High Priest." This is such a common coin that Jesus already knows the inscriptions that are on it.) The questioners bring the coin to Jesus, and He asks them about its image and the inscription. The delegation says that the image and inscription on the coin belong to Caesar.

This narrative leads up to Jesus' pronouncement that the things that belong to Caesar should be given back to Caesar, and the things of God should be given back to God. The coin with the image belongs to Caesar; so Jesus says that what belongs to Caesar should be given back to Caesar. The term for giving back here is different from the term used in the delegation's question to Jesus. The question makes it appear as though the tax paid by the Jew was a gift. Jesus' answer indicates that the tax is not a gift but what is actually due, that is, it must be given back to Caesar. Jesus does not satisfy the Jew who does not want to pay taxes. He says that Caesar has a legitimate place, but God does also. When Jesus says that the Jew should give back to God the things that are God's, He is saying that Caesar is not divine and should not make such a claim. Jesus supports the Jews who do not like the coinage with the image and divine inscription. There is to be a clear separation between Caesar and God. It should also be clear to Jews that God is superior: Caesar is not divine.

Many have used this Scripture erroneously to build a doctrine of absolute separation between church and state. The point of this Scripture is the supremacy of God. While the separation of church and state has positive elements, we can be thankful that it has not been strictly adhered to in our country's history: our coins have the inscription, "In God we trust," and God is mentioned in the pledge of allegiance to the flag. Ideally, Israel was a theocracy until the Jews wanted a king like the other nations. However, we as Christians live as citizens of two realms. Our ultimate loyalty is to God, and this text concerning taxes points us to God as supreme.

The Christian is taught in Romans 13 and 1 Peter to cooperate with government because all governments have authority from God. This means there can never be equality between God and the state because God is the state's source of authority and is superior to it. Mark's audience is being persecuted by governmental authorities, and it is interesting that Mark includes this story. Being persecuted does not allow anyone to avoid responsibilities to the state, which includes the payment of taxes. Even while paying taxes, however, we must acknowledge the superiority of God over every government.

The delegation is impressed by Jesus' answer. They marvel at Him because Jesus has given them an answer that cannot be disputed.

The Question About Marriage (12:18-27)

As the Pharisees and Herodians leave, the Sadducees come. The Sadducees, the wealthy, ruling, priestly class, are mentioned only once by Mark. They had several beliefs that ran counter to the Pharisees. They accepted only the five books of Moses as legitimate Scripture, and they derived their beliefs only from those books. They rejected the concepts of resurrection and angels.

The Sadducees do not have a trick question for Jesus, but they do not expect Him to give a serious answer to their question, even though they address Him as "Teacher" (Mark 12:19). They want to show how ridiculous the idea of resurrection is by the question they ask. The Sadducees introduce the situation by referring to a practice called levirate marriage, which is discussed in Deuteronomy 25:5-10, a passage the Sadducees accept as canonical since Moses wrote it. Because property was so important, it was imperative for a man to marry and have children who could inherit his property. If a man died without children, his brother was allowed to take his widow in marriage so that children might be born who could inherit the deceased's property. The children of the brother's marriage were legally considered to be the children of the dead man. The practice is also referred to in Genesis 38 and in Ruth.

Having brought up the subject of the levirate marriage law, the Sadducees propose a ludicrous situation in which a man marries and dies without having children. The man has six brothers who all perform their marriage duty according to the levirate law, but all die before any children are born. Finally, the widow dies! The legal question asked by the Sadducees is, "At the resurrection [when they rise again] whose wife will she be?" (Mark 11:23). This is not a political issue as in the Pharisees' question, but a theological question framed in the scribal debate style. The Sadducees want Jesus to align himself with them against the Pharisees and show that the resurrection idea is ridiculous. It may be that they mock Jesus and the resurrection at the same time.

Jesus is more harsh with the Sadducees than with the Pharisees. Jesus says that they are deceived in two ways: first, the Sadducees do not really know the Scripture. Second, they do not know the power of God. Jesus first dispenses with the overt question concerning marriage in Heaven by denying any marriage in Heaven and stating that when people get to Heaven, they will be as the angels. This is a twofold blow to the Sadducees since they deny both Heaven and angels.

Then Jesus turns to their unasked question concerning the reality of resurrection. Jesus says that the dead are raised and asks the Sadducees if they have ever read the book of Moses. (Remember that earlier they quoted from the books of Moses!) This illustrates Jesus' point that they are Scripturally ignorant. They use Scriptures for their own purposes and not for knowing God. Jesus then quotes Exodus 3:6, when God speaks to Moses out of the burning bush and identifies himself as the God of Abraham, the God of Isaac, and the God of Jacob. These leaders had been dead for some time at the time of this identification, but God had always promised deliverance to those who keep covenant with Him. That covenant was not simply deliverance in this life, but for the life with God, which is endless. Therefore, God will still keep covenant with those men and will raise them.

It is ridiculous to think of God as being a God of the dead. He is God of the living because He is the initiator of life. The Sadducees deny the power of God. They acknowledge His creation of life, but they will not allow God to have the power to create life from the dead. Which is easier: to create life in the beginning, or to put life back into a person who is dead? The Sadducees assumed that God can give life once but not twice. How ridiculous! Jesus has turned the ideas of the Sadducees upside down. He concludes the questioning session by saying again how deceived the Sadducees are (Mark 12:27).

The main lesson for Mark's church is that they have the assurance of God's deliverance in times of persecution when death may be imminent. The living God is the God of the living. This incident gives us further assurance of the resurrection. We will have a different kind of life in the resurrection, but it will be a life everlasting. We should be careful in our speculation concerning further details about what it will be like in Heaven.

The Sadducees' lack of Scriptural knowledge, misuse of Scripture, and their denial of the power of God is a lesson we should not miss. We must know the Scriptures and read from them what the message of God is, rather than read into Scriptures what we think we already know. The denial of the power of God is also a contemporary problem. For us to determine what God will or will not do—or what He can or cannot do—is presumptuous. Just because we do not think it is possible does not mean that it is impossible for God, even in our modern world. Do not be deceived. Study the Scriptures and acknowledge the power of God.

The Question About the Greatest Command (12:28-34)

Both the Pharisees and the Sadducees employed scribes who were professionally trained to interpret the law. This time, it is a scribe who asks Jesus a question. He overhears Jesus' answer to the Sadducees and notices how well Jesus answers their baited question. Since Jesus' answer is so sensible, the scribe reasons that Jesus might tackle a difficult question that is hotly debated among Jews: what is the first of all the commands? (The question was not a debate about which commands should be obeyed and which could be ignored; all 613 commands had to be obeyed!)

The question concerns which of the commands is the best summary of the intent of the whole law. Hillel, a prominent Jewish rabbi, once had been challenged by a Gentile to summarize the law. He replied, "What you hate, do not do to your neighbor. This is the whole law. All the rest is commentary. Go and learn it." Jesus meets the challenge by repeating the Shema, which is very nearly a Jewish creed. (The orthodox Jew repeats the Shema—a combination of Deuteronomy 6:4-9; 11:13-21; and Numbers 15:37-41—twice a day.) Jesus only uses the first part of the Shema, from Deuteronomy 6:4 and 5. "The first command is that you should love the Lord God with all your heart, soul, mind and strength" (Mark 12:29, 30, A.T.).

Jesus prefaces the command with Judaism's unique statement that the Lord God is One. This monotheistic statement is the presupposition for the commands that follow. The oneness of God was in sharp contrast to the polytheistic nature of Mark's Roman audience and the population around Palestine. It is only on the basis of this oneness that love for God can be commanded. The fourfold expressions of wholeness (heart, soul, mind, and strength) represent the whole person. It is inappropriate to attempt to distinguish between them. The command is to love God with all that one is.

However, Jesus does not summarize the whole of the law in one command. Jesus wants the scribe to know that there is a second command that is also important: love your neighbor as yourself. Jesus states that there is no other command greater than this. The second command comes from Leviticus 19:18. Some Jews would have agreed with Jesus, but seldom would they have put these two commands together. Jesus places them in tandem because the basis of our love of neighbor is our love for God. Love for God comes first, and then we are able to love our neighbor.

The first-century Jew understood the concept of neighbor to mean his fellow Jew, but Jesus does not make that distinction. The parable of the good Samaritan, which follows these commands in Luke 10, makes clear that the concept of neighbor transcends ethnic and religious barriers. Nor does Jesus commend self-love when He says to love your neighbor as yourself. To love one's neighbor as oneself means we are to love others as if we were in their place. For example, the good Samaritan loved the wounded Jew not because he loved himself, because if he had loved just himself, he would have left the area as soon as possible, just as the priest and Levite had done. The good Samaritan loved the Jew and put himself in his place. Therefore, he spent his time, energy, and resources because he loved the Jew as he loved himself, that is, as though he were himself in that situation.

When the scribe realizes the wisdom of Jesus' answer, he acknowledges it by repeating the answer in his own words (Mark 12:32, 33). His repetition is not exact. The scribe typically omits the sacred name when he says, "There is One." (The NIV translation, "God is one," misses this point.) He also adds his understanding that there is none other except Him. This addition is from Deuteronomy 4:35. He repeats the idea of wholeness, leaving out "with the whole soul" because the Septuagint omits that phrase. The scribe agrees with the second command also, and adds his understanding that this is more important than whole burnt offerings and sacrifices. (Whole burnt offerings were sacrifices that were totally burned, while other sacrifices were partly burned and the remainder eaten either by the priests or the person making the sacrifice. This distinction was well known among Jews.) Hosea 6:6 says, "I delight in loyalty rather than sacrifice, and in the knowledge of God rather than burnt offerings" (NASB).

The scribe is unusual. His question is not to entrap; rather he commends Jesus' answer and agrees with it, and he is commended by Jesus for answering with such understanding. Jesus states that this man is not far from the kingdom of God. The scribe is close to the kingdom of God because he understands Jesus' priorities and because he is in close proximity to Jesus. What the scribe lacks is a commitment to follow Jesus. The time comes when the

Jews are unable to deny the miraculous signs that Jesus does, but at the same time they refuse to accept the implications of those signs that point to Jesus as the Son of God.

This section has several clear lessons for Mark's church and for us. Jesus did not reject Old Testament law, but He did reject the scribal interpretation of the law. The two great commands are valid for the Christian. Paul summarizes several of the Old Testament commands by the new command to "love your neighbor as yourself" (Romans 13:8-10). It was the Pharisaic attempt to circumvent the commands and nullify the intent of the law that brought Jesus' wrath. We tend to keep some New Testament commands according to the letter but avoid the intent. Sometimes we try to decide who our neighbor is and whether we should help. We are like the priest and Levite who passed by on the other side, all the while rationalizing their actions.

The first great command also teaches us something about the wholeness of our response to God. One of the misconceptions about tithing is that if we give ten percent to God, then the rest is ours to do with as we please. Jews and Christians should not compartmentalize life. We must love God and obey God with all our heart, soul, mind, and strength—not with ten percent, but with one hundred percent. We must realize that there are many in our neighborhoods and congregations who are not far from the kingdom of God. They know the right answers and live appropriately, but have simply not made the commitment to act. What should our response be to these people?

No one else dares to question Jesus after the scribe's question (Mark 12:34) because Jesus has demonstrated His teaching power and His authority. The scribe acknowledges Jesus' authority, but it is also an opportunity for Jesus to respond with a similar kind of question, knowing that the scribes who are present will not be able to respond with a ready-made answer.

Jesus Questions the Scribes' Hypocrisy (12:35-44)

Jesus, having answered their questions, asks the scribes something that is designed to confound these legal experts. How can the Messiah be the son of David if David, in Psalm 110:1 speaking to God, refers to the Messiah as his Lord? How can David's Lord be David's son?

The scribes believe that the Messiah is from the line of David. The Old Testament teaches this in Isaiah 9:2-7 and Jeremiah 23:5

and 6. In Mark, we have the blind beggar crying out to Jesus as the "Son of David" for deliverance (Mark 10:47, 48), and in the triumphal entry, the crowds cry out, "Blessed is the coming kingdom of our father David" (Mark 11:10). Jesus is traced through the lineage of David in the genealogy written in Matthew and Luke. The idea of the Messiah as a descendent of David was well known, as well as the idea of David as the great military leader who built Israel into a powerful nation.

The popular idea of one like David coming to deliver the Jews from foreign powers was consistent with the idea of the Messiah coming from the lineage of David. But as Jesus points out in Psalm 110:1, David through the Holy Spirit says, "The Lord said to my Lord: 'Sit at my right hand until I make your enemies a footstool for your feet.' " In this quotation, the first word *Lord* in the Hebrew text is the four-consonant word for God, *YHWH,* sometimes translated "Jehovah." The second word *Lord* is *adonai,* which is best translated as "Lord." Thus, we have God speaking to the Lord of David saying, "Sit at My right." The scribes must have recognized this as a Messianic Psalm, otherwise Jesus could not have made His point. The Psalm paraphrased reads: "God said to the Messiah, my Lord, sit on My right." The right side of God indicates the power to rule in the name of the ruler. The next step in the argument-question, then, is if David calls the Messiah "Lord," and he does, then how can David's Lord be his son? The scribes cannot answer Jesus, much to the delight of the crowd (Mark 12:37).

Jesus rejects the popular view of Messiah. He does not deny that the Messiah is from the lineage of David, but He asserts that the Messiah is much more. Jesus says that David is not the proper lineal model for Messiah. The Messiah's kingdom is not like David's kingdom because there is a major difference in quality. The Messiah is like David, but not in the military sense: Jesus crushes His enemies not by warfare, but through His death on the cross. This Messiah is not like David because the Messiah sits at the right hand of God. Although the Messiah is from David, He is even more because He is from God. The Christian understands that only when the Messiah/Son of David is resurrected to God's right hand can He be both the son of David and Lord of David. (The Messiah is the son of David by lineal descent and the Lord of David by the resurrection.) The scribes cannot understand this, but this concept is precisely what Peter preaches on the day of

Pentecost (Acts 2:34-36) when he quotes from Psalm 110:1 and then proclaims the truth that God has made Jesus both Lord and Messiah.

Mark begins this section with the scribe's question to Jesus about the great command and the scribe's commendation. Then Jesus stuns the scribes when He asks the question about the son of David. In the following text, Jesus condemns the scribes for their ostentation.

While Jesus is in the temple teaching, He warns His listeners about the scribes. The warning is not against their teaching, but against their actions. The warning is not directed toward all scribes, but toward those who (1) like to walk around in long robes, (2) like the greetings in the marketplace, (3) like the first seats in the synagogues, (4) like the first places at banquets, (5) devour the houses of widows, and (6) pray for a long time in pretense.

The scribes wore long, white linen robes. This was the traditional garb for teachers, but some scribes wore excessively long robes with fringe so that they would be noticed.

Matthew 23:7-10 refers to the greetings in the marketplace. The designations *Rabbi, Leader,* and *Father* are mentioned and were popularly used to address religious leaders.

The first seats in the synagogue were benches placed just before the chest holding the Torah. Scribes seated on these benches faced the audience and were highly visible.

The first seats at the banquets were next to the host. The host and his special guests were served first and were served the best food. Jesus says that it is not simply the robes, greetings, or first seats that are wrong, but that the scribes spend their efforts to achieve deferential treatment. Jesus condemns their presumption and ostentation.

The scribes also "devour widow's houses," but the meaning of that expression is obscure. Scribes could not accept payment for their teaching, but they could accept hospitality and gifts. Since they had no job other than teaching, scribes were supported by others. Perhaps they were "devouring widows' houses" by taking advantage of vulnerable widows and their hospitality and literally "eating them out of house and home," as we say today.

The final mark of ostentation has to do with the scribes' habit of making long prayers. It was a common practice for Jews to pray by themselves but in public places. Jews still practice this method of public prayer. Various shrines in Israel are visited by orthodox Jews, especially for the purpose of prayer. The Wailing Wall in Jerusalem attracts Jews every day of the year. Jesus' condemnation is not against public prayers, but against lengthy public prayers that are uttered in pretense so that others will think the ones praying are very religious. The attempt by scribes to deceive others about their spirituality is especially dangerous because they may deceive themselves into believing that they are really praying.

Jesus says that these scribes will receive great judgment (Mark 12:40). The best parallel is James 3:1, where James says that many should not teach because they will be judged with a great judgment. The scribes and teachers will be judged more strictly because they are the ones teaching others.

Teaching occurs not only by what one says, but perhaps even more by what one does. It is crucial that the teacher not only speak the right words but also live them. The scribes Jesus describes teach properly, but their prayers and public life are only for show and not for the worship of God.

This warning against pretense and ostentation in religious life is certainly applicable for today. The use of distinctive religious attire, special spiritual titles, and preferential seating for certain people in church services or at banquets is still prevalent. The question that should be resolved is the motivation behind the conventions. Are the robes, the titles, and the important seats sought for personal gain, or are they given for recognition of personal work for the sake of the kingdom? We must not get caught in the trappings of personal benefit and glory. We must also be wary of those who do their religious work simply for the show.

After a strong condemnation of the showy practices of the scribes, Jesus teaches His learners the contrast. While sitting opposite the treasury box in the court of women in the temple, Jesus observed the crowd throwing in their copper coins into the thirteen trumpet-shaped boxes used to collect monetary gifts for the temple. Jesus observed many rich people throwing in much money. Jesus does not commend or condemn these givers, but a certain widow, obviously very poor, comes and catches His eye. When she contributes two small copper coins, Jesus calls His learners together to teach them.

Jesus says that the widow has thrown in more money than all the rest of the people. This is mathematical nonsense if we are comparing actual monetary units. Jesus, however, explains His mathematical reasoning in percentages. The other people threw their surplus money into the treasury box while the widow put all her coins into the temple treasury, an amount that represented her whole living. She contributed from her need, while the rest contributed from their surplus. Jesus does make mathematical sense if we look at percentage giving.

The scribes count only what is on the outside; so Jesus counters with this pictorial lesson designed to teach a spiritual reality. Note that Jesus proposes no gospel of prosperity in this incident. The widow does not prosper through her actions even though she has given sacrificially.

The incident of the widow's giving is a summary of what Jesus has been teaching the learners since He revealed His approaching death. The widow would normally be thought of as being last, but Jesus has made her first. The widow gives her whole living, and Jesus tells His learners that their whole lives must be committed. The heroine is one of the poor for whom Jesus shows special concern. Jesus comes to seek and to save the lost, not those who think they can find their own way. This incident again shows Jesus' reversal of common values. It is not the amount, but the commitment behind the gift that matters. And finally we see the widow in sharp contrast to the self-seeking scribes.

The learners hear what Jesus teaches, but they often do not grasp His concepts. Immediately after this pictorial lesson when Jesus stressed the beauty of a poor woman's gift to the temple, the learners and Jesus leave the temple and the learners are impressed by the richness and beauty of its wonderful stones and buildings. Jesus' lesson has not been fully understood.

CHAPTER ELEVEN

End Times

Mark 13:1-37

Chapter thirteen is an enigma to some Christians because the meaning is cloaked in apocalyptic form, and because of its extended length. Apocalyptic language uses visual imagery, numbers, catastrophic events in the heavens and on earth, and animal symbolism. Apocalyptic material is popular in times of depression and persecution because it promises the end of the world with God triumphant over all. Apocalyptic material is written as an encouragement to the reader.

Normally, the book of Mark contains only short narrative sections. (Chapter 4, about the parables, and this apocalyptic chapter are the only exceptions.) The author utilizes the longest narrative section in this chapter.

Although the language in this section is apocalyptic, this section of Mark differs from the norm because it emphasizes warning and gives very little instruction or encouragement. The main grammatical feature of the chapter, which is uncommon in apocalyptic material, is the warning feature. There are seventeen imperatives used in the chapter, and most of them are utilized as warnings. Most apocalyptic material is written in the first person and not the second person imperative.

Another important feature of this section is its occurrence in the context of discussing the temple. Jesus has just completed teaching in the temple when the learners ask Him about the beautiful buildings of the temple. Immediately after this chapter, Jesus is anointed for His death, burial, and resurrection. He is tried partly because of His declaration concerning the destruction of the temple and His ability to raise it in three days. (We know, of course, that this is a reference to His body and not to the literal temple.) The temple was a subject earlier in Mark when Jesus cleared it because the people had made it a den of thieves. Now

He describes the destruction of the very temple He had earlier cleared (Mark 13:5-23).

There is also a confusion in this chapter between the destruction of the temple and the coming end of the age that is signaled by the coming of the Son of Man. The learners ask when this will be and what the sign will be concerning the destruction of the temple. The learners believe that the destruction of the temple will be a sign of the imminent end of the age. The four paragraphs talk alternately about the destruction of the temple and the coming of the Son of Man, which will occur at the end of the age.

There is also a confusion in Mark's church (the temple has been destroyed and the end of the age has not yet come) concerning the nearness of the end of the age. We share with Mark's church the paradoxical tension that acknowledges that the end is soon, but not yet. The end has always been "soon, but not yet." There are signs, but no one knows; so this apocalyptic section's purpose is not to inform about the signs of the end of the age, but remains a warning to be vigilant and to watch.

With this in mind, let us explore this chapter following the outline below:

1. The learners admire the temple, and Jesus replies about its destruction (Mark 13:1, 2).
2. The inner circle asks privately when this will happen and what the signs will be (Mark 13:3, 4).
3. Eight warnings of the destruction of Jerusalem (Mark 13:5-23).
4. The coming of the Son of Man in the clouds (Mark 13:24-27).
5. Signs that the destruction of the temple is close (Mark 13:28-31).
6. No signs for the coming of the Son of Man; therefore, watch (Mark 13:32-37)!

The Learners Admire the Temple, and Jesus Replies About Its Destruction (13:1, 2)

The situation occurs when Jesus and the learners leave the temple and the learners make remarks about the greatness of the stones and the buildings. Jerusalem's temple had been constructed by Herod during the early years of the first century B.C. and was not yet complete when it was destroyed in A.D. 70. The temple had massive columns that were about twenty-seven feet high and seventeen feet in circumference. The building was a large, irregular quadrangle (with sides measuring about 1560 feet, 877 feet, 1462 feet, and 1040 feet) with the sanctuary (100 feet by 50 feet) within another building area (341 feet by 536 feet). The outer area included a court for the Gentiles. The inner area included a court for the women. Some of the white building stones were twenty-five feet by eight feet by twelve feet. The building was a beautiful sight and an architectural wonder.

Jesus predicts the total destruction of the temple: not one stone will be left on top of another. There are two main reasons from God's point of view why the temple should be destroyed. First, the temple had been seriously corrupted by the Jews. Second, the temple with its sacrifices were a part of an old agreement with the Jews that would no longer be valid in the new agreement because Jesus was designated the final and ultimate sacrifice. The temple was no longer to remain a part of God's plans.

The Inner Circle Asks Privately When This Will Happen and What the Signs Will Be (13:3, 4)

After the learners leave the temple, they cross the Kidron Valley and climb to the top of the Mount of Olives. From this point they can look back at the city and have a complete view of the temple area. The inner circle (Peter, James, John, and this time Andrew) come to Jesus privately for an explanation of His earlier remarks. They ask two questions. First, "When will these things be?" They want to know when the destruction of the temple will take place. At this point in their education, the learners view the destruction of the temple as a catastrophe and a sure sign of the end of the age. The second question concerns their desire to know what the signs will be when the temple will be destroyed and the end of the age will come.

Eight Warnings of the Destruction of Jerusalem (13:5-23)

Warning One — Look Out for Those Who Will Come in My Name (5, 6)

Jesus does not answer their question. Rather, He warns them against people who have easy answers to that question. There will be persons who will pose as the Messiah, and they will lead people away from the truth. The coming of false messiahs is not a sign of the end; it is only a warning that some will claim that the end is here because they are the messiah. Jesus' warning is do not be deceived by such people. When such people come, you will know the end is not yet. You will need to continue to keep watch and to proclaim the good news.

Warning Two — Do Not Be Disturbed (7, 8)

The inevitable wars and reports about wars, with nations and kingdoms battling each other, as well as earthquakes and famines are not signs of the end. The end is not yet. These signs are only the signs of the beginning of the end. These signs, which most Jews would conceive as the signs of the end, are only affirmations of the beginning of the end. There is no time sense in Jesus' remarks. Jesus wants His learners not to be disturbed when they hear about these events because He wants them to continue their proclamation of the good news.

Warning Three — Look Out for Yourselves (9, 10)

What is about to be said has no reference to the end, but to what will happen to the learners of Jesus. The persecution of Jesus' followers is not the end. Likewise, the persecution of the readers of Mark's book is not a sign of the end. The persecution of the learners and Mark's church are simply continuations of the persecution that followed Jesus and led to His death. It is an inevitable part of Christianity, not necessarily a sign of the end. The learners will be delivered to local Jewish courts and be convicted. The learners will be whipped in the synagogues because of their conviction. The learners will stand in court before foreign rulers and kings on account of Jesus. It is clear that this persecution is simply a continuation of the persecution that Jesus endured. (See Acts 9:5.)

It is clear from Acts and the letters of Paul that persecution of Jesus' followers was continued by the Jews. Paul was whipped at least five times and stood trial before several Jewish and Roman officials because he proclaimed the good news. The point of this warning is that the followers of Jesus should expect persecution. Persecution is not a sign of the end of the age. Rather, it is an opportunity to continue to testify about the good news. This message is to be delivered to the rulers and kings before whom any learner is brought. It is the delivery of this message that brings the learner before rulers and kings. The good news must be proclaimed to all the nations despite arrests, beatings, and trials. In fact, the trials are opportunities to further proclaim the good news. Verse 10 indicates that it is necessary for the good news to be proclaimed. This necessity is God's way of letting people know the good news concerning His Son.

Warning Four—Do Not Be Anxious About Speaking (11-13)

When you are brought to trial, do not be concerned about how to defend yourself. Instead, allow God's Spirit within you to provide the words in order to proclaim the good news. Jesus is giving His learners assurance that not defending themselves (Jesus did not defend himself) will actually aid them in the proclamation of the good news.

The aid of the Holy Spirit does not mean escape from persecution. Brother will betray brother to death; a father will betray his child to death; children will stand up against their parents and have them put to death; and followers of Jesus will be hated by others because of the name of Christ, which they confess. But the one who endures to the end will be delivered: courts may convict, authorities may whip, and kings may kill—but God will ultimately deliver and vindicate the ones who are continuing to trust in Him.

Again, these persecutions are not signs of the end, but they provide opportunities for proclamation. The persecutions that will follow the ones who testify to Jesus are normal. Mark's audience should expect suffering and persecution if there is proclamation, and so should we. The comfort in persecution is that the end of persecution brings deliverance to the one who has been trusting God, and destruction to the persecutor. (See Philippians 1:28.)

Warning Five—Let the Reader Understand (14-17)

Some translations regard the phrase, "Let the reader understand" (Mark 13:14) to be an aside to Mark's audience, but this should be understood as a saying of Jesus concerning one who reads Daniel. Daniel 9:27 is the source of the expression "desolating sacrilege" (Mark 13:14, A.T.), which was a reference to the sacrilege by Antiochus Epiphanes when he slaughtered a pig in sacrifice on the Jewish altar. But Jesus refers to the destruction of Jerusalem or to the desecration of the temple by the zealots during the Jewish war against the Romans in A.D. 66-70, which precedes the destruction of the temple. Some in Mark's audience might see the "desolating sacrilege" as an individual such as Nero who claimed divinity.

This warning is a curious combination of third person imperatives contrasted to the second person imperative warnings in the rest of the chapter. This section is a predictive warning to those in Jerusalem just prior to the destruction of the temple and the city itself. Besides the command to understand, there are four others: let the ones in Judea flee to the mountains, let not the one on the roof come down, let him not go into his house to pick up anything, and let not the one in the field return to pick up his overcoat. These, along with the lament concerning women who are pregnant or nursing children, are indications of the urgency to get away. Drop everything and run. Do not bother even to pick up a coat because the destruction is so close.

This is not an indication of the end. There would be no sense to flee if the end were coming for all the world. It is only the end of Jerusalem. Normally in a war, one would flee to the walled city like Jerusalem for security; so these warnings are doubly significant because the people are to flee to the mountains—away from the city. (There are references in Eusebius that many Christians fled from Jerusalem prior to its destruction and went to Pella.)

Again the message is that these signs, destructive and catastrophic as they are, are not signs of the end, but merely signs of the destruction of Jerusalem and the temple.

Warning Six—Pray (18-20)

This is a continuation of the prior warning indicating that the misery will be great. And as great as the misery might be, it would be even worse if it occurred in the winter because the rains make travel very treacherous during that season. Everyone would be destroyed in this destruction if the Lord had not shortened the time. This is an indication that even in times of great misery and affliction, God is still in control for the sake of His selected followers because they are trustful to the end.

Warning Seven—Do Not Trust (21, 22)

When someone says, "The end is come," "Christ is here," or, "Christ is there," do not trust that person. Before the end, there will be many false messiahs and false prophets who will do wonders and signs. Do not follow these people. They will say the end has come, but remain steadfast and do not trust these people. With all the urgency, with all the great misery, the end is not yet.

Do not be deceived by false people, even those who claim to perform wonders and signs.

Warning Eight — Look Out (23)

This section is a summary and echoes warning number one. Watch, be careful, do not be deceived—because Jesus has told you before that all these things will happen. What Jesus has not told is when and what the signs will be. This section says that although the end is certain, it is not yet, and the normal signs of the end are not signs of the end of the age. Even the destruction of the temple is not a sign of the end of the age. Therefore, we should not watch for signs because we can misinterpret them. Instead, we should remain watchful so that we are not deceived by false messiahs or prophets. We must continue to proclaim the good news until He actually comes again.

The Coming of the Son of Man in the Clouds (13:24-27)

This brief section, totally made up of Old Testament texts, is not a reference to the destruction of the temple. The destruction of the temple was to precede what is being described in these verses. This section does not describe a sign of the end; it describes **the end** itself, since the coming of the Son of Man in the clouds signals a new age. The affliction that is mentioned in verse 24 is a reference to the preceding events that come before "those days," an allusion to the end time, which culminates in "that day" (cf. Mark 13:32) or the "day of the Lord." The darkening of the sun and moon, along with the falling of the stars, are not literal events. The shaking of the powers in heaven is a summary of the sun, moon, and stars—everything that lights the heavens—which lose their light.

This apocalyptic language is used to describe a meaningful reality. In the ancient world, most people believed that gods and goddesses controlled the celestial bodies. When the Son of Man comes, God intervenes in history and the celestial bodies are eclipsed. History ends. The meaning of the failure of the celestial bodies concerns this intervention by the Son of Man. Coming in clouds and with great power and splendor are allusions to the divinity of the Son of Man. The clouds, power, and splendor all belong to God in the Old Testament.

In Daniel 7:13, the Son of Man is presented to God, but in this passage, the Son of Man carries the power and splendor of God and performs the work of God as He sends messengers out to gather together the selected ones. (See Deuteronomy 30:3; Isaiah 43:6.) Just as God promised in the old agreement to bring all Israel together, the Son of Man sends out messengers to gather all of God's people at the end. They are to be gathered out of the four winds and every corner of heaven and earth. All are to be gathered.

Because the destruction of the temple might seem to be a defeat for God, Jesus tells of the ultimate triumph of the Son of Man and gives assurance to His learners (and to Mark's audience) that the destruction does not mean that God has lost. The Son of Man concept that is stated here is in sharp contrast to the Son of Man's humiliation in Mark 8:31. This is why we often speak of a second coming: the first coming was in humiliation, but the second coming is in great power and splendor. But the same Son of Man comes (or came) both times.

Signs That the Destruction of the Temple is Close (13:28-31)

Jesus returns to the question asked by the inner four. When will this be and what will be the signs? Jesus gives them the signs only after He sternly warns them not to be deceived by false messiahs, persecution, and catastrophic events, even the destruction of the temple. These events will occur, but they are not the signs for either the destruction of the temple or the end of the age. Immediately after giving the signs (Mark 13:28-31), Jesus returns to the warning mode by repeatedly telling the learners to look out, keep awake, and be watchful. This section concerns not the end of the age, but the timing of the end of the temple.

Jesus encourages the learners to learn the lesson of the fig tree. Late in the spring, a fig tree puts out its leaves and everyone knows that summer is near. The emphasis on *near* means that the things occurring are before the end. Therefore, since the events of verses 24-27 are the end, those of verses 28-31 must concern time before the end—in this context, the destruction of the temple. Note also that the expression *these* in verses 29 and 30 refer back to the *these* and *all* of verses 4, 8, and 23, which are concerned with the destruction of the temple and not the end of the age.

The emphasis in this lesson is not on chronological time, but on sequence and the sureness that events will happen. Persecution occurs, then the destruction of the temple. It occurs in this precise sequence and it will surely occur. When the learners see these things happening, they will know that the destruction is near, even at the door. Again, the emphasis is on sequence and the surety that what Jesus says will indeed happen. Some translations incorrectly have the expression *"He" is near* (Mark 13:29), referring to the Son of Man's coming. The Greek text allows either *it is near* or *He is near*. But in context, since the passage is talking about the destruction of the temple, the former is the proper translation. This becomes very clear in verse 30, since the events will take place before that current generation dies.

Jesus begins the saying about the generation with a strong affirmation of its truthfulness. If Mark was written shortly after the temple destruction in A.D. 70, then this saying is a continuation of the assurance that God does what Jesus says He will do in His own sequence and time. This is the assurance that is given again in verse 31, when Jesus says that heaven and earth may go away but His words will not go away. Jesus' answer to the learner's question is that the temple destruction is near and signs of deception, persecution, treachery, and affliction will precede its destruction. The learners are not only informed but assured that these events will take place. This is double assurance for Mark's audience because they know that God has destroyed not only the temple but also Jerusalem. Therefore, they have assurance He keeps His word, and the end of the age will also come.

No Signs for the Coming of the Son of Man; Therefore, Watch (13:32-37)

The chapter ends by repeating two expressions: *no one knows* (Mark 13:32, 33, 35), and the warnings, *look out* (*be on guard*), *keep awake,* and *watch* (Mark 13:33, 35, 37). *That day* is a reference to the Day of the Lord or day of victory or vindication. "That day" comes after "those days" of verse 24, which depicts the end; therefore, this section also deals with the end of the age. When Jesus says that no one knows the day or hour, He refers to the end of the age; He had just given some signs about the end of the temple. Jesus is emphatic that no one knows, adding that the messengers in Heaven do not know, even though they are the ones who will be sent out to gather the select of God from the four corners of the world. His emphasis is heightened further when He says that even the Son does not know! (Jesus, as the Son of Man who is coming, does not know when He is coming.) That statement alone ought to be enough to silence persons who dare to say they know when Jesus will return or predict when He might return. It is presumptuous to assert that one knows facts that Jesus does not know. The truth is that only the Father knows.

Since this is true, the learners' only alternative is to Look out! Keep awake! For they do not know when the time is. *Look out* is a continuation of the warning from verses 5 and 9. *Keep awake* is a new imperative, meaning in our current idiom, "Do not go to sleep on the job." This is the point of the parable of the man who leaves his home and puts his servants in charge, with each having work to do. The command to the doorkeeper is to "watch." This identical word is used in Mark 14:34, 37, and 38. It means to keep awake. Metaphorically, the word means the same as the *keep awake* in verse 33, that is, do not go to sleep on the job. Each servant not only has authority, but each has his task. The word was not simply to watch for the master's return, but to work at whatever job one has so that when the master returns, the work is done. *Watch* is not a command to search for signs so that one can figure out what no one but God knows. It is a command to do the work that God has given.

The parable repeats the watch command in verse 35. "You do not know when the master of the house will come back" (A.T.); therefore, your work should be done. The master might come at any time, including any of the four watches of the night. The learners are commanded to watch or to keep at their work so that when the master does return, He will not find anyone sleeping. The passage should not be taken literally and so does not ban sleeping. We must understand it in a metaphorical sense, that is, do not go to sleep on the job. In other words, keep up the good work. The concluding verse expands Jesus' warnings to the inner four to include all persons. "What I say to you, I say to everyone: 'Watch!' " The time is unknown, but the fact is that He will come; so we must watch.

This chapter is an assurance for Mark's audience that the end has not yet come, no matter what others might say. When the end comes, everyone will know. No one knows the time, but it will be soon; so the task of the learner is to keep awake by proclaiming the good news to all nations. Just as suffering preceded Jesus' resurrection, suffering precedes the follower's ultimate resurrection.

The lessons for us are clear. We know the end is certain, but we do not know when it will happen. We know our obligation is to keep awake doing the work of proclamation of the good news to all nations. It is human nature to long for signs because we want to know exactly when the end will be, but if we knew when the end would happen, we would be relieved of the necessity of staying alert. We could simply set an alarm clock and wake up in adequate time to prepare for the awesome event. The point of watching is not to figure out when, however, but to continue proclaiming the good news until it is no longer necessary to do so.

WATCH!

CHAPTER TWELVE

Death Draws Near

Mark 14:1-52

The final three chapters of Mark are often referred to as the "Passion Narrative" because they relate the suffering of Jesus, but this title emphasizes the wrong event. These chapters actually relate the fulfillment of the three previous predictions that Jesus had made concerning His death, burial, and resurrection. His death, burial, and resurrection are the core of Christianity: these events constitute the good news. The idea that suffering and death can mean good news is a seeming anomaly, but Jesus' death becomes a part of the good news when His empty tomb proclaims Him as the resurrected Lord. These three chapters contain the history of the preached good news, which is the history of Jesus' death, burial, and resurrection. Mark's purpose in relating these events to his church is to give them the history behind the good news (gospel) that they are to proclaim. The historical reality of these events is also important to us, because our trust not only lies in the existential present, but is firmly grounded in the reality of historical events.

Death Plot (14:1, 2)

The Passover was a one-day festival that occurred just before the seven-day Festival of Unleavened Bread. In Jewish writings, these feasts were often referred to interchangeably by either designation. Preparation for the festival began early in the day so that everything would be ready when Passover began at sundown. All leavenings had to be discarded from every household. The lambs and goats were sacrificed in the afternoon, and their blood was drained and thrown upon the altar. Then each carcass, complete with head and legs, and with no bones broken, was given to the worshipers. Each worshiper came home and roasted the lamb in preparation for the Passover meal, which occurred after sundown. The participants dressed in white and reclined around the table for the repast. The meal was prepared as a great memorial of Israel's redemption from slavery in Egypt. It is therefore symbolic that Jesus, the lamb of God, was killed at the same time as the lambs were for the Passover meal.

The chief priests and scribes were already seeking to arrest Jesus and kill Him because He threatened their power and authority. They meant to arrest Him quickly and quietly without undue notice. John 11:57 indicates that the rulers had already advertised that they wanted to arrest Jesus. The leaders, however, were not anxious to arrest Jesus during the Passover and the Festival of Unleavened Bread because Jerusalem was filled with crowds who had come to participate in the festivities. Many in the crowd could have been Galileans and might be favorable to Jesus. Some scholars speculate that as many as 200,000 additional people were in the Jerusalem area during these festivals. The Roman garrison routinely was reinforced during the season to quell potential disturbances. In addition, the Jewish zealots would be more active during this period because they would remember their subjugation even while they were celebrating their earlier escape from Egypt. The rulers rightly suspected that arresting Jesus with crowds present could precipitate an uncontrollable riot.

Anointing for Burial (14:3-9)

Mark interrupts his narrative concerning the rulers' plot to destroy Jesus and the role that Judas played in it with a second narrative concerning a woman who anointed Jesus with perfume. This is another occasion where Mark's interruptions are meant to teach the readers. The woman's gift is in startling contrast to the treachery of Judas. Jesus' comment to the woman about anointing His body for burial is a demonstration that Jesus knows that He is about to die even though His enemies do not yet have firm plans.

There are several occasions of anointings in the gospels, and each is unique. This anointing is singular because the woman anoints Jesus' head, and because it occurs just two days before His death. The scene is in Bethany at the home of a leper named Simon. He must have been well known to Jesus and His learners, but he is not mentioned elsewhere in the Scriptures. Jesus is eating at the table when the woman enters, breaks an alabaster jar, and pours perfumed ointment of pure nard over Jesus' head. Nard is

ed from a plant that is native to India; so her gift is very
sive.

re are two reactions to the woman's behavior. Mark de-
s the action of "some" (Mark 14:4). Matthew 26:8 makes it
that the "some" were the learners close to Jesus. The learn-
e indignant; they feel that the valuable ointment has been
d. (An estimate of the perfume's value is three hundred
ii, which—at that time—was about equal to a year's wages
working man. At today's minimum wage, the sum would
almost $7,000.) The learners conclude that it would have
better to sell the ointment and give the proceeds to the poor.
indicates that the learners lash out at the woman because
see her action as a monstrous waste of money.

us reacts in sharp contrast to His learners. The giving of
to the poor was a major aspect of Jewish piety. Jesus' com-
that the poor are always with us is not meant to cause us to
at it is hopeless to help the poor because they will always be
Jesus' emphasis is in the words *always* and *not always*. Jesus
not always" be with the learners; therefore, the woman has
something good for Jesus. Jesus will soon be gone, but the
will remain, and ways to help them will "always" be avail-
while Jesus will not always be available.

us tells His learners to stop bothering the woman and not to
her trouble. The woman did not realize that Jesus would
be gone and that she was anointing Him for burial. The
ers' comments to her could well have made her remorseful
she had not sold the ointment and given the proceeds to the
(Had she known what events were coming, she might have
to use the proceeds to "save" Jesus, which also would have
impossible.)
an assurance to the woman, Jesus tells her that she has done
she could, and that it was a good work she did for Him.
story is similar to the story of the widow who threw her
e living into the treasury box. Apparently, the woman who
ted Jesus also gave Jesus all that she had, and this was a
work because the anointing was in anticipation of Jesus'
l.) The woman simply meant to honor Jesus with an anoint-
a common occurrence in greeting people for a meal. (See
7:46.) At this point, Jesus not only indicates that He knows
eath is imminent, but He uses this occasion to remind His
ers once more that He is about to die.

Jesus further commends the woman by saying that the incident will be spoken of as a memorial to her whenever the good news is proclaimed in the world (Mark 14:9). The woman's memorial is not in our remembering her name but in remembering her deed (her name is never mentioned). This verse also indicates that Jesus is aware that His death will end in resurrection because He knows that the good news of His death and resurrection will be proclaimed throughout the world and, in that proclamation, this woman's deed will have a place. The woman becomes an example of following for Mark's church and for us. She gives what she has. She stands in strong contrast to the learners who criticize her "wastefulness" and do not understand that Jesus must soon die, and in even stronger contrast to the particular learner who decides to betray Jesus to the authorities.

Judas Begins His Betrayal (14:10, 11)

Judas, aware that the authorities want to arrest Jesus, decides to cooperate with them. Mark describes Judas as one of the Twelve. Judas has been with Jesus from the beginning. There is speculation why Judas makes such a tragic decision: is he greedy for the payment he will receive, does Satan make him helpless to resist temptation, or is he simply zealous and trying to force Jesus to show His power? Perhaps he is afraid at the turn of events and is trying to cooperate in order to help himself.

Judas' motivation remains unknown, but Mark notes that the chief priests are delighted (Mark 14:11). They are so pleased that they promise to give Judas payment in silver coin. For his payment, Judas will have to lead the authorities to Jesus when Jesus is not in a public place. This deception indicates that the rulers know they will cause a riot if they try to arrest Jesus publicly. It also indicates that they know that they do not have a plausible case. Another contrast between Judas's actions and the woman's is that her ointment was worth about $7,000, while Judas received only thirty silver coins (about $700) for his betrayal.

The Passover Celebration (14:12-25)

Preparation for Passover (12-15)

The Passover Feast and the Feast of Unleavened Bread were so connected that often either title was used to indicate both feasts. The Feast of Unleavened Bread was to be celebrated the seven days following the Passover, but because the Jews were to eat unleavened bread during the Passover meal (Exodus 12:8), all of the leaven had to be removed from their homes prior to Passover. (Technically, the day before the evening when the Passover started was not a day of the Unleavened Bread Feast; but since preparation for both feasts had to occur before the Feasts, the title applied, as in Mark 14:12, to the day before the feasts.) Even the Passover preparation of the sacrifice of the lamb had to be completed before the celebration, which Mark also notes in verse 12.

The learners want to know where they can prepare the feast. Because this is a Passover meal, it has to be eaten within the walls of Jerusalem. Therefore, they cannot travel to their friends' home in Bethany as they had done each evening earlier in the week. Jesus gives them instructions that are similar to the instructions He had given them to prepare for His earlier entry into Jerusalem. On this particular occasion, it appears that Jesus has made prior arrangements. Since the Jewish leaders seek to kill Jesus and He wants to celebrate the Passover before they seize Him, it is important for Jesus to cause little notice regarding His movements.

Jesus sends the learners into the city to find a man carrying a ceramic jar and tells them to follow the man to a house. It would be easy to find the man carrying a jar because that was normally a woman's task, while men carried wineskins. The learners are instructed to ask the master of the house, "Where is my guest room, where I may eat the Passover with my disciples [learners]?" (Mark 14:14). Notice the possessive *my* before *guest room,* and note that the upper room that the learners are shown has already been furnished and prepared for the feast. The room's preparation would have included rugs that covered the floor and low couches that would be used for people to recline around the table. Preparation also included tableware and lamps, since this meal would continue late into the night. Perhaps the master of the house also would have supplied the unleavened bread and wine. But it remained for the learners to prepare the roasted lamb and the special dishes of bitter herbs and mixed stewed fruits. The two learners then rejoin Jesus when all the preparations are complete.

Prediction of Betrayal (16-21)

Jesus arrives at the upper room with the Twelve just after sunset. They recline and begin to eat the celebration meal. The initial Passover feast was hastily eaten by persons who wore shoes and robes, ready to depart at a moment's notice, but throughout the years, celebration tradition decreed that even the poorest Jew should be able to relax and recline at this meal, a recognition that the meal was a celebration of Jewish release from captivity in Egypt. Passover meals had become leisurely and lengthy occasions.

Mark's narrative, true to form, is brief and to the point. As soon as the dinner has begun, Jesus makes a startling announcement that someone who is eating at the same table with Him will betray Him. The learners are shocked. The irony of Jesus' being betrayed by one of the Twelve, and especially by one who eats at the same table, is reflected in the learners' responses when they exclaim, "It is not I, is it?" They are dismayed at the idea of betrayal. They do not accuse each other, but question Jesus concerning themselves, but the way each one frames his question indicates that they all expect a negative response from Jesus. Jesus, however, does not answer their questions, but simply repeats His announcement using different words.

There is probably a reflection of Psalm 41:9 in Jesus' announcement. Psalm 41:9 indicates that a close friend who even ate at the same table as the psalmist had turned against him. The emphasis centers around the importance of table fellowship to the Jews. Jews do not eat with persons who are not intimate friends; so Jesus' announcement that His betrayal will be initiated by one of His close associates around the feast table is shocking. Despite the implicit denials in the learners' immediate response, we must realize that, ultimately, it is not only Judas who betrays Jesus, but all of His learners (Mark 14:27-31, 50).

The death of the Son of Man is inevitable, but that fact does not excuse the person who initiates the betrayal. It may seem curious that although the death of Christ means salvation for those who accept Him, the one who precipitates that death by betrayal has still committed a grievous wrong and will be judged accordingly. Jesus pronounces a woe on such a betrayer.

These two sections mark the passage that turns a typical Jewish Passover meal into the Christian eucharist. Jesus is portrayed by Mark as the lamb who is to be sacrificed. The Passover also indicates that God's deliverance from Egypt has now a new deliverance that is also within God's plan, for the Son of Man goes as it has been determined. Mark shows the betrayer to be one of the learners who has been with Him constantly and eaten at the same table. Mark shows that Jesus is aware of the betrayer, but does nothing to prevent His betrayal.

As the Christians listen to the reading of Mark's book, they also understand Mark's message that they should not fail or betray Jesus after eating with Him at the Lord's Supper, or behave like the band of learners who scatter when Jesus is seized. This is certainly a contemporary message for us who gather so regularly around His table to participate in the commemoration of Jesus that we call Communion. We should not be found betraying Him by our words or our actions so soon after we have eaten with Him.

New Meaning at Passover (22-25)

The host at the Passover meal is usually the head of the house. Jesus assumes the function of the host, and the meal progresses in the regular way. The meal is served, but before it is eaten, its various components are explained. The bread is unleavened because the Jews had to leave Egypt in haste. The bitter herbs represent the bitterness of their captivity, and the lamb represents the blood that was spread on the lintel as a signal for God to pass over the house when He brought death to the firstborn in Egypt.

When Jesus takes up the loaf of bread to begin the meal, He first says a blessing on God for His provision. Then, breaking the loaf, He distributes it, adding words of interpretation similar to the words of interpretation for the Passover elements. However, Jesus makes His learners aware that what He says is a new element: the bread represents not a broken Jesus, but Jesus himself and His presence with the followers.

Since breaking a loaf of bread is the usual way a Jewish family began a meal, the practice of blessing, breaking, and distributing bread will become a daily reminder to the learners about Jesus' last meal with them and that He promised He would be with them. If we understand the phrase *this is My body* as meaning, "This is My life," then we realize that Jesus gave His life over to death on behalf of many.

It is also true that the act of eating the bread, a token of Jesus' sacrificial life, becomes a way of vicariously sharing His sacrifice, just as in the Jewish tradition where most sacrifices were eaten either by the priests or by the one who brought the sacrifice. The believer shares in the blessings of Jesus' sacrificial death by sharing the broken bread. While Jesus' words explaining the Passover elements relate to the deliverance of the Jews from Egypt, His words about the bread and cup anticipate His sacrifice as a deliverance to many who will be bound by a new agreement.

Somewhat later during the meal, either at the drinking of the third or fourth cup of wine, Jesus gives another new interpretation. He begins with a prayer of thanksgiving. The Greek word for thanksgiving is transliterated "Eucharistia," which has become the liturgical name of the rite of Christian Communion. This term, *thanksgiving,* also reflects the concept of joy and celebration that was a prominent focus of the early Christians' meals. Jesus' interpretation is, "This is My blood of the agreement which is poured out for many" (Mark 14:24, A.T.). The cup or "poured out blood" represents Jesus' violent sacrificial death. (See Deuteronomy 19:10 and Matthew 23:35, where poured-out blood means violent death.)

An agreement was sealed by the sacrificial blood of an animal (Exodus 24:8) and is referred to as the blood of the covenant. So the learners anticipatively partake in the blessings of the new agreement that is sealed by Jesus' violent death. They do this by drinking the cup of wine that represents His soon-to-be-poured-out blood.

The last phrase, *for many,* refers to the fact that His imminent death is on behalf of many. A similar expression occurs earlier in Mark 10:45, where Jesus represents His mission as giving His life as a ransom "for many." The sacrifice and cup are for all people, not just for the Jews. Jesus' death is a vicarious death because He died in the place of others. Those who drink the cup include themselves in the "many" and thus appropriate the deliverance that God provides through His Son.

The solemn affirmation that Jesus will not drink the fruit of the vine (Mark 14:25) is very strong. First, He begins with the "Amen," which indicates an important teaching; then the solemn vow has three negatives in a row. In effect, Jesus says, "I will no longer not not drink ... until I drink it new in the kingdom of God." The next cup Jesus drinks is the cup of suffering and death. (Note that Jesus refuses to drink the wine offered to Him while He is hanging on the cross; Mark 15:23.)

"Drinking it new" is often thought to refer to the end time at the marriage feast of the lamb (Revelation 19). But it is sensible to understand that if Jesus has simply resolved to drink the cup of suffering and accomplish God's will, then in His next meeting with the learners after the resurrection, He will eat and drink with them in the same intimacy of table fellowship to which they were accustomed. It is interesting to note that a meal occurs in almost every resurrection appearance.

Mark is brief as always. There is no mention of other Passover elements. Mark's church is familiar with the bread and cup. It appears that Mark wants the church to be aware of the past, present, and future sense of the Lord's Supper. It is clear that, in partaking, we look back to the cross where His violent death occurred on our behalf. It is equally clear that we are to realize that He is present in table fellowship. We are present with Him, not only in the reenacting of His death, but as we bring the meaning of His death into our lives.

We participate in meal fellowship with Jesus as we have participated in the deliverance Jesus accomplished by His death. The meal fellowship is to continue into the future until He comes again and all Christians from all time will sit together at the Messianic marriage feast of the lamb. The early church prayer "Maranatha" was the closing prayer at the Lord's supper. Come, Lord Jesus!

Because bread and wine were common elements for most meals, the early Christians ate these foodstuffs daily and were continually reminded of Jesus' death and resurrection. It is unfortunate that we have separated the Communion elements from daily sustenance and relegate them for use in special worship services to remember Jesus' sacrifice. It is appropriate for Christian followers to remember the elements of the good news whenever they eat together or eat similar food and drink.

We also need a greater emphasis on the present and future sense of the Lord's Supper. We should recognize Communion as a solemn remembrance of Jesus' death, but we should realize that it is also a joyous celebration that He is not dead but has risen and is surely coming again!

Another important aspect of the Lord's supper that we neglect is the intimacy of table fellowship. Eating together declares our commonality and oneness: eating alone is a graphic illustration of isolation. Our current practice tends to be far too individualistic for the health of the church.

Jesus Predicts Denial and Desertions (14:26-31)

The Passover meal ends with the singing of the Hallel, which is Psalms 114—118. Jesus and His followers then leave the city and go out to the Mount of Olives. It is while they are walking that Jesus predicts that the learners will all stumble. The classical Greek word used here carries the idea of being lured into a trap, while its use in the New Testament generally means to sin. To demonstrate the truthfulness of His statement, Jesus quotes Zechariah 13:7 concerning the shepherd's being struck and the sheep's being scattered. Although this is a despairing note, Jesus assures His followers that He will be raised up and go before them into Galilee. Jesus recognizes that what He is about to undergo, He must do by himself. Jesus also recognizes that although He faces a violent death, He will gain resurrection. There is despair, but there is also hope. Mark's readers—who are also facing persecution—will see this same lesson. There may be despair ahead in terms of persecution, but there is a resurrection. The scattered sheep will be gathered again when the shepherd will go before the sheep and lead them into Galilee. The promise of a post-resurrection appearance in Galilee is repeated by a messenger at the tomb (Mark 16:7).

This section is very similar to Jesus' earlier three predictions of His death and resurrection. The learners hear His words but react only to the possibility of His death. They do not understand His reference to resurrection. Peter maintains that although everyone else is lured away, he will be steadfast. Peter has not heard the hope word of *resurrection*. Jesus replies by predicting Peter's threefold denial. Jesus literally says, "Today, this night, before the rooster crows, you will absolutely deny Me three times" (Mark 14:30, A.T.). Jesus is clear—the denial is imminent and complete, and not once but three times. Peter is equally adamant, as he uses a double negative to say that even though he may be threatened with death, there is "no way at all by any means" that he will deny Jesus. All the learners agree with Peter and echo his statement. Jesus knows that the death of the others has no salvific value; so He does not encourage their line of protest and repeats, without rancor, His statement that they will desert Him.

This section is a warning to Mark's persecuted church against their undue brashness. Christ alone has the power to endure; so He alone must be our shepherd. We cannot and should not depend upon human direction.

Jesus Prays While the Learners Sleep (14:32-42)

The small company has reached a place called Gethsemane, which means oil press. John describes this place as a garden that is located beyond the brook Kidron on the Mount of Olives (John 18:1). Since Judas soon appears, we presume that this is a favorite place of Jesus or that Jesus had previously told the learners, including Judas, that He wanted to spend some time there after the Passover meal. It is an open place. Jesus asks most of His learners to sit and wait for Him while He walks ahead in order to pray.

Jesus takes only the inner three along, and He expresses His anguish to them. The three words used in this section to describe Jesus reflect great anxiety and grief. The human side of Jesus is apparent during the next few sections. Jesus is very troubled because He knows what will happen. Although He knows that His resurrection is certain, He also knows that the terror and torture prior to His triumph will be just as real. Jesus tries to tell the inner three about His grief by referring to Psalm 42:6 to describe His feelings. Jesus desires some company during His trouble, but He is destined to be alone. He asks these inner three to stay where they are and to keep awake, being watchful. Jesus goes ahead a short distance and falls prostrate on the ground and begins to pray concerning His approaching hour of suffering.

Jesus addresses God familiarly with the Aramaic word for father, *Abba,* which is somewhat equivalent to our word *Daddy.* Jesus is aware that all things are possible with God. The expressions *hour* and *cup* are similar references. The cup represents the wrath of God that is rightly poured out upon the disobedient. The vicarious nature of Jesus' death is pictured because He takes the cup and drinks from it; that is, He suffers and dies. The prospect of facing God's wrath over sin troubles Jesus even as He accepts it. Jesus' ultimate prayer request is not removal of the cup, but that God's will might be done, not His own. Jesus is willing to obey even though He can predict the terrifying events that will happen to Him. Obviously, His death on the cross was no accident; it was the plan and will of God from the beginning, and Jesus was willing to be obedient.

One answer to Jesus' prayer comes when He returns to His inner three and finds them sleeping. Jesus is totally alone. His followers are not able to stay and keep awake with Him. Jesus wakes them and addresses Peter particularly. "Keep awake and pray so that you will not enter into temptation," He says (Mark 14:38, A.T.). Jesus shows concern for His followers even in His own time of suffering. Their temptation will be coming soon in the form of desertion and denial, but these men who so recently swore that they would go to the death with Jesus are not able to keep awake with Him for an hour of prayer. Earlier, these learners had said that they were willing to drink the cup of suffering from which Jesus has prayed for release. The learners do not know what the cup and loyalty will cost them, and they ultimately desert when the inevitable pressures materialize.

The statement that the spirit is willing but the flesh is weak may allude to Psalm 51:12. If so, then the spirit is God's spirit and reflects Jesus' real struggle since He was human (in the flesh) and certainly had a willing spirit.

When Jesus walks back to the learners between His second and third prayers, only to find them asleep, the learners simply do not know what to say (Mark 14:40). But Mark points out that this has been their reaction much of the time as Jesus tries to explain His mission and purpose. (If they could not keep awake and pray with Him for one hour, they could hardly be expected to remain with Jesus when His arrest and death become obvious.)

"The hour has come," Jesus says (Mark 14:41). The event toward which He has been moving for some three years is about to happen. Just as He had predicted, the Son of Man is about to be betrayed into the hands of evil people. Jesus urges the learners to go meet the person who is about to betray Him.

Mark's church has an example before them of Jesus' obedience and the failure of the learners. Jesus is our exemplar, not Peter or any other human. Obedience is the key even in times of persecution. Our prayer in persecution should not be, "Deliver me," but, "May Your will be done." Our tendency is to pray only for deliverance.

Judas Betrays Jesus and the Learners Flee (14:43-52)

As the previous section indicates, Jesus goes to meet the persons who are looking for Him. Mark states that Judas, the betrayer, is one of the Twelve. This, along with the kiss, shows the treachery of Judas' betrayal.

The crowd behind Judas, sent from the Jewish leaders who want Jesus' death, comes armed with short swords and wooden clubs. The crowd includes the temple police plus some of the slaves and servants of the chief priests and scribes. Judas has told the group that he will kiss the one whom they want to arrest.

Because so many people in Jerusalem might have known or seen Jesus at some time, we wonder why a signal kiss is necessary. But in the darkness outside of the city, Judas does not want the crowd to make a mistake and arrest the wrong person; so he comes to Jesus with the normal greeting of a learner to his rabbi. He calls out, "Rabbi!" and then kisses and embraces Him. Seeing the agreed-upon sign, the crowd moves in, seizes Jesus, and starts to take Him away. The treachery is complete because the greeting, the kiss, and the embrace signify betrayal disguised as love.

One of the followers who is standing by (John identifies the person as Simon Peter—John 18:10) draws someone's sword to fight off the crowd and, in the struggle, cuts off an ear of one of the high priest's slaves. Jesus restores the ear in Luke's account (Luke 22:51), but Mark simply continues his narrative with Jesus' protestation against such a crowd's coming to arrest Him with swords and clubs, especially since He has been readily available to them in the temple each day. His statement probably does not refer so much to the swords and clubs—the crowd surely expected more defensive response from the learners than they received—as to their coming in secret. Jesus points out that the crowd is just as treacherous as Judas since they decide to arrest Jesus away from the crowds who heard Him so gladly in the temple.

When Jesus says, "Let the Scriptures be fulfilled" (Mark 14:49, A.T.), He may be referring to the fact that His arrest, conviction, and crucifixion are all a part of His mission and purpose, which have already been determined by God. This is the event for which He was born. But the fulfillment of Scripture may also be a reference to the Zechariah passage quoted in Mark 14:27, which concerns the shepherd who is struck and the sheep who are scattered. As if in fulfillment of that Scripture, Mark simply notes that the learners all abandoned Jesus and ran away into the darkness (Mark 14:50).

Verses 51-52 tell about a specific person who had fled. A young man who had been following along was also seized by the crowd, but he had quickly pulled away. In his movements, stepped out of his clothing, a long linen cloth. Why does Mark include this vivid incident while the other three Gospels are silent? There is much speculation that the event signifies some form of typology (for example, Joseph, who flees Potiphar's wife) or the analogy of another young man who is found sitting in the empty tomb. More likely, it is Mark's eyewitness account about himself. If so, this passage indicates that Mark followed Jesus and the learners after they ate the Passover meal, which was likely held at his home. Mark's mother seems to have been wealthy enough to own her own home and had a residence large enough to permit the early church to meet together for prayer (Acts 12:12). The linen cloth is unusual because most clothing typically was made of wool. Only the wealthy were able to afford linen material for their garments.

CHAPTER THIRTEEN

Crucifixion and Resurrection

Mark 14:53—16:20

Jesus Is Tried, Condemned, and Insulted (14:53-65)

When Jesus is brought before the high priest, all of the Sanhedrin (chief priests, elders, and scribes) assembles for the spectacle. The Sanhedrin functions as the supreme council for Jewish religious and political matters. Jesus' appearance in court is part of an initial hearing to establish whether there is sufficient evidence to hold Him for trial. In fact, a formal trial never occurs because the Sanhedrin abdicates their authority in favor of the Roman law under Pilate, the Procurator for Judea.

During this hearing, the Sanhedrin looks for testimony that will require a death sentence for Jesus. They initially find no such testimony, although false witnesses are plentiful. The testimony of the false witnesses either does not indicate the severity of capital punishment or the testimonies do not sufficiently agree with each other. In serious crimes requiring capital punishment, it was necessary to have two or three witnesses whose testimony would agree (Deuteronomy 17:6). Even the accusation that Jesus said He would overthrow the handmade temple and then in three days build another not made with hands was not corroborated by a sufficient number of witnesses. According to John 2:19, Jesus did say something similar, but the witnesses cannot agree. An accusation of disrespect for the temple was serious and would have brought condemnation. See Acts 21:28, for example: when people believe that Paul has desecrated the temple by bringing a Gentile inside, the crowd attempts to kill him for his heinous act.

Finally, the high priest asks Jesus why He is not answering the testimony against Him, but Jesus remains silent. Then, seeking to trap Jesus, the high priest asks the most direct question possible. "Are you the Christ, the Son of the Blessed One?" (Mark 14:61). In Jesus' time, Messianic pretenders were commonplace; so the high priest wanted to test Jesus with this question. Up to this point, Jesus had avoided using Messianic references to himself in public teaching. However, Mark's audience was aware that Jesus was the Messiah from the very beginning of the book. The secret was a secret no longer: Jesus states very clearly, "I am." (Jesus had kept this fact a secret in order to enable Him to continue His teaching and preaching until He reached Jerusalem.)

If Jesus had stopped talking after uttering two words, the Sanhedrin would have only had another heretic to incarcerate, but Jesus continues: "You will see the Son of Man sitting on the right hand of Power and coming with the clouds of the heaven" (Mark 14:62, A.T.). The high priest understands Jesus' meaning: "Son of Man" is Jesus himself. The high priest recognizes Jesus' reference to himself as sitting on the right hand of Power (a paraphrastic for God) as blasphemy of the highest order. No one can appropriate the privileges of God. The expression "coming with the clouds of heaven" (see Psalm 110:1 and Daniel 7:13) is probably not a reference to the end time, but simply a continuing reference to being with God.

The high priest rips his robes, a sign of disturbance and indignation, because he has just heard outrageous blasphemy. God's name has been dishonored by a man who puts himself beside God. There is no further need for witnesses: the Sanhedrin has already determined that Jesus certainly is not the Son of God, and therefore, He has condemned himself by blasphemy. The Sanhedrin unanimously condemns Jesus, making Him liable to die for His crime. It is ironic that the outcome the rulers cannot accomplish through false witnesses is accomplished by Jesus when He speaks the truth.

This section demonstrates again that Jesus is in control, not the Sanhedrin. The death of Jesus is not an accident, nor is it the result of illegal trials or political intrigue. Jesus' death is planned and inevitable.

The actions of spitting and beating (Mark 14:65) are prominent in the Old Testament and indicate dissociation from the wrong actions of another. (See Deuteronomy 25:9.) If the Sanhedrin council participated in these actions against Jesus, then they were dissociating themselves from Jesus and His so-called blasphemy and were showing their contempt for Him. Other Gospel accounts indicate that it is the soldiers who blindfold Jesus and taunt Him by asking Him who is hitting Him when they know He is not able to see. Even the attendants who were with Peter earlier join in the fun and games and strike Jesus.

Mark in this narrative makes it clear that although Jesus is going to be crucified, He is not guilty of a crime other than claiming to be who He really is: the Christ, the Son of God. Being a Christian in Mark's time, then, is not being a follower of a criminal, but proclaiming allegiance to the Son of God.

Jesus' behavior is a powerful example of how to face persecution and trials. Mark's church, in the midst of their own persecution, will recall that Jesus suffered humiliation, beating, and finally death. The church will remember Jesus' resurrection and claim that promise if they also suffer. The next section shows them the opposite way to face persecution.

Peter Denies Three Times (14:66-72)

Peter had begun his denial process when he ran away as Jesus was arrested. Although Peter had followed behind the group that had seized Jesus, he was far enough away so that he could not be mistaken for a follower. But his curiosity made him come closer when he reached the location where the Sanhedrin was meeting. In fact, Peter ventured into the inner courtyard and sat down by a fire to warm himself against the cold night air.

The servant girl's first accusation is made after she observes Peter very carefully. The girl's statement, made directly to Peter, associates him with the man who is being tried by the Sanhedrin. Her statement can be taken as derogatory because she refers to "the Nazarene," which means someone who is not from Judea.

Peter does not directly deny the girl's statement. He is evasive and maintains that he neither knows nor understands what she says (Mark 14:68). But Peter's behavior shows how uncomfortable he is; just as he had run away for fear of his life earlier, this time he retreats from the warm fire and the group in the inner court to the outer courtyard. The servant girl pursues him and this time makes her accusation concerning Peter to those standing in the outer court. She asserts that Peter is "one of them" (Mark 14:69), meaning that he is one of the followers of the man who is on trial. Mark simply comments that Peter denies her accusation again (Mark 14:70).

All three denials occur in a very short time period. The third accusation comes, according to Mark, "after a little while" (Mark

14:70). The accusation comes from those who are standing around the outer courtyard. These are the people the servant girl had earlier told about Peter. Apparently Peter's speech patterns or accent has singled him out because they accuse Peter of being one of the followers because he is a Galilean in accent. Matthew 26:73 notes that it was Peter's dialect that betrayed his home country.

Peter's final denial is absolute. He first invokes a curse upon himself if he is lying (and, by implication, a curse on his accusers if he is telling the truth). Peter also makes a solemn oath. Both the curse and the solemn oath are Peter's attempt to convince the crowd that he is truthful when he says that he does not know the man. This is a direct denial of Jesus—and immediately the rooster crows. Peter then sadly remembers what Jesus had predicted, and he breaks down and cries.

This is perhaps the most critical application passage for Mark's church. They were facing persecution as Christians. If they were brought to court, they would be accused of being followers of Jesus in the same way as Peter had been accused. The incident regarding Peter's denials is a stern warning to them against denial and the bitterness it causes. But the story relates an indication that there is also forgiveness. Mark's church knows Peter was a great leader in the early days of the church; so they acknowledge that even though he had earlier denied knowing Jesus, he was later fully forgiven. Mark 16:7 indicates this fact when the messenger mentions Peter by name.

Our denials of Jesus are not made in the face of persecution and are usually not verbal denials. Our denials are more behavioral; we deny Jesus by our actions while we affirm Him in our words. We should be careful that both our words and our actions express loyalty and commitment to Jesus.

Mark's church sees, as we also see, the vivid contrast between Jesus, who does not deny His identity when He is faced with death, and Peter, who denies his Master when he is faced with pressure. But even with Mark's warning against denial, we see the grace of God at work in forgiveness. The contrast between the denials of Peter and Judas is also clear: both cried bitterly for their error, but Judas cut himself off from the hope of forgiveness through suicide. Judas could also have gained God's forgiveness had he chosen to ask.

Trial Before Pilate and Humiliation (15:1-20)

A new theme, kingship, arises rather suddenly in this chapter. Jesus is not mentioned as king until this chapter, which refers to Him as such on six different occasions. He is also mocked as a king by the soldiers in words and actions when they give Him a purple cloak, a crown of thorns, and a fake scepter, and finally when they kneel and worship Him. All references to Jesus' kingship are made by His opponents (Pilate, the soldiers, or the shouting crowds).

Although no one, including Pilate, takes the claim that Jesus is a king seriously, it is the main charge that Pilate centers on and displays above the cross as Jesus' crime. *King* is not a title Jesus would have used for himself, but, in reality, the title is apt. Jesus really is king, but Pilate and the Jewish leaders reject Him and kill Him. The legal allegation of being a pretender king was a political accusation, and was untrue. But from a theological viewpoint, Jesus really is king of the Jews because He is the Messiah. Jesus' identity as king illustrates another paradox: Jesus is accused correctly of being king of the Jews, but those who accuse Him do not actually believe that He is king of the Jews.

Jesus' Trial Before Pilate (1-5)

The Sanhedrin has already sealed Jesus' fate, but early in the morning, with the whole council, they decide to turn Jesus over to Pilate. It may be that the whole council has not met in the middle of the night and that some of those more favorable to Jesus, such as Joseph of Arimathea and Nicodemus, were not there. They decided to turn Jesus over to Pilate because, although they could condemn a man to death, they did not have the authority to carry out the sentence. Executions were the prerogative of the Roman government.

The Sanhedrin knew that their accusation would have to be altered in order to induce Pilate to execute Jesus. Pilate would not execute a person for religious reasons; so the council decides to change their accusation and charge Jesus not with blasphemy, but with treason, for which execution is the common punishment. The council then puts Jesus in chains and hands Him over to Pilate for judgment.

Pilate begins his interrogation of Jesus by asking Him whether He is the king of the Jews. Pilate does not believe the accusation, otherwise he would have had Jesus executed without hesitation.

Mark shows clearly that Pilate acknowledges Jesus' innocence. Pilate knows that it is envy that motivates the chief priests to turn Jesus over to him (Mark 15:10). Later, just before he turns Jesus over to be crucified, Pilate asks if there is any evil that Jesus has done. Jesus' only reply indicates neither an acceptance nor a rejection of the title king. Jesus only makes this one comment and the earlier acknowledgment before the high priest that He is the Christ and will sit at the right hand of God. Other than these remarks, Jesus is silent during the trials despite the urgings of both the high priest and of Pilate. Mark reflects again the suffering servant theme of Isaiah 53, especially verse 7:

> He was oppressed and afflicted,
>   yet he did not open his mouth;
> he was led like a lamb to the slaughter,
>   and as a sheep before her shearers is silent,
>   so he did not open his mouth.

The chief priests make other charges against Jesus; Jesus still does not respond. Pilate invites Jesus to give answers and marvels when Jesus remains silent. Perhaps Mark intends this attitude of Jesus to be followed by those in his church who are brought before Roman judges during their present persecution. There is no need to answer false charges, but only to acknowledge the truth.

This section also assures Mark's readers that although Jesus was executed as a criminal, He was in fact innocent of any wrong. On the contrary, it is Jesus' accusers who are wrong. Jesus is also the example to Mark's readers that the innocent do suffer and that not everything is set right in this world.

The Question Concerning Barabbas (6-15)

Jesus was not the only criminal on trial that morning. We know that at least two others were condemned. It is likely that Barabbas was also due to be executed. Barabbas was a revolutionary, probably a zealot, who wanted to overthrow the Roman government. In his fight against the government, he had killed people and was in prison for these crimes. Barabbas's followers are in the crowd at the trials to see what will happen to their leader. Since they are aware of the Roman custom of releasing a prisoner during the Passover festival as a way of keeping some peace and showing generosity, they ask Pilate to continue the custom. Pilate, seeing a chance to allow Jesus to be released, asks whether they want their king to be released. Pilate knows that Jesus was before him only because of the envy of the chief priests. But the chief priests incite the crowd to have Pilate release Barabbas instead. Barabbas's followers certainly want him released, and Barabbas himself was probably something of a folk hero whom many of the Jews secretly admired because he defied the Romans. Now Pilate is in a quandary; so he asks the crowd what he should do with Jesus, their king. Mark shows Pilate to be a crowd pleaser, and since he has let the crowd decide Barabbas's fate, he also allows the crowd to decide Jesus' fate (Mark 15:12). Probably Pilate did not expect the cry for blood that arose from the crowd. Crucifixion was an execution reserved for the worst of crimes because it meant humiliation and a slow, painful death. But the crowd wants crucifixion! Pilate is astonished and asks what Jesus has done to deserve such a death. The crowd's only reply is, "Crucify him!" (Mark 15:14). Pilate, the crowd pleaser, releases Barabbas; he has Jesus scourged with leather thongs tied with bits of bone and metal as a prelude to crucifixion; then he releases Jesus to soldiers to be crucified (Mark 15:15).

The irony of the situation cannot have been lost on Mark's readers. A real traitor to Rome, a murderer, is released while an innocent man wrongly accused of being a traitor is condemned. Barabbas is freed while Jesus is crucified. Mark might also want to illustrate the picture of how a sinner who comes to Jesus is freed because of the death of Jesus. As sinners, we deserve God's judgment; but as Christians, we know that Jesus has taken that judgment upon himself.

History has shown that many Jews have suffered at the hands of Christians because the Jews are blamed for causing the death of Jesus. But to place blame for the death of Jesus on the Jews overlooks a number of important points. First, Roman authority actually carried out the sentence. Second, Jesus' purpose and mission was to die; so we cannot blame the Jews. Jesus deliberately went to Jerusalem, cleaned out the temple, allowed Judas to betray Him, and refused to call angels to defend Him in Gethsemane. One of Mark's themes in this passion narrative is that Jesus is in control at all times. Third, Jesus' death brings life to us; therefore, His death has excellent results. Fourth, if it were not for our sins, His death would have been unnecessary. Thank God that Jesus did die for our sins that we might have life eternal!

Mocking of the Soldiers (16-20)

There can be no other purpose for this section than to demonstrate the absolute and utter humiliation that is heaped upon Jesus. After Jesus has been convicted of being the king of the Jews, the soldiers lead Him out of public view into an inner court of the palace of the Roman governor in Jerusalem, called the Praetorium. Having called the rest of their battalion (upwards to 200 men), they decide to make fun of Jesus according to His conviction as king of the Jews. They begin their mockery by throwing a purple cloak around Him and weaving for Him a crown made of thorns; then they greet Him with the same greeting generally reserved for Caesar, but they say, "Hail, king of the Jews" (Mark 15:18). The soldiers take the reed, which Matthew describes as a scepter, from Jesus' right hand and begin to hit Him with it. The final ironic ignominy occurs when they kneel and mockingly worship Jesus. It is a humiliation beyond understanding, but Jesus accepts it without protest. Cruel and brutal humiliation was an integral part of death by crucifixion; Roman citizens convicted of a capital crime were allowed to die quickly and honorably by beheading.

Everyone around Jesus mocks Him: the Sanhedrin, Pilate, the crowds, the robbers on either side, the people passing by, the soldiers, and even His disciples, who mock Him by their desertion. Note that each group mocks Jesus in a different way. The attendants of the chief priests mock Jesus as a prophet, the crime for which the Sanhedrin has convicted Jesus. The soldiers mock Jesus as a king, the crime for which Pilate has convicted Jesus. Jesus is alone!

The Crucifixion (15:21-41)

Jesus has been so weakened by the trials, beatings, and mockery that He is unable to drag the cross beam for His cross; so the Roman guard compels a passerby named Simon to carry it for Him. Mark inserts the names of two sons of Simon of Cyrene. These names are only mentioned in Mark, which must mean that Mark's readers would know both Alexander and Rufus. Rufus may be the same person greeted by Paul in Romans 16:13.

Jesus' weakness is further indicated by the fact that He died so quickly on the cross. Pilate was surprised and tells the guard to check and make sure He is dead before He will release the body to

Joseph. Sometimes a person would take two to three days to die on a cross.

The soldiers bring Jesus to Golgotha, which is Aramaic for "Place of the Skull." We do not know the origin of the term. It could refer to the shape of the hill or, perhaps, to the fact that this was the execution ground. The place is outside the city and yet close to the road for passersby to view the execution and take warning not to commit similar crimes.

The wine mixed with myrrh (Mark 15:23) was a type of drug to dull the pain. Mark does not say who tries to give the drink to Jesus, but we can assume that it must have been some of the women. It would be out of character for the soldiers who had so recently inflicted such mockery and punishment on Jesus to want to relieve His pain. This was a custom perhaps from Proverbs 31:6, which admonishes the reader to give strong drink to the one perishing. This incident, as well as several others, also reflects fulfillment of some Old Testament prophecies, as in Psalm 69:21. Jesus refuses to drink, perhaps because He had pledged not to drink wine until He drank it new with His learners in the kingdom. Others suggest that Jesus meant to suffer fully in order to atone for the sins He had taken on behalf of all people.

The soldiers crucify Jesus. In crucifixion, the arms are stretched on the cross beam and either nailed or tied. The cross beam is then attached to the upright pole and the feet are nailed to the upright pole. Then the whole cross is lifted up and set into a hole, and the person being crucified is left to die. The soldiers began the process around the third hour (Mark 15:25), which is about 9:00 A.M. The official notice of Jesus' crime, "King of the Jews," was nailed on the cross above Him. This was to act as a deterrent to others thinking to commit the same kind of crime.

Two robbers are also crucified, one on either side of Jesus. These two are probably zealots and compatriots of Barabbas. This is another fulfillment of the suffering servant chapter of Isaiah, which says, "He . . . was numbered with the transgressors" (Isaiah 53:12).

Jesus' total possessions consist only of His clothes, and these become the property of His executioners. Unwilling to agree upon a proper division, the soldiers throw lots to see who will receive which parts of Jesus' clothing. This also fulfills prophecy (Psalm 22:18). After dividing Jesus' clothing among themselves, the soldiers settle back to watch and wait for His death.

The mockery does not stop with the soldiers. People who travel down the road wag their heads, a sign of derision, and taunt Jesus with the accusation that was used at His trial before Caiaphas, the high priest. If Jesus is powerful enough to destroy the temple and rebuild it in three days, surely He is able to save himself from the cross!

The chief priests make the most of their victory and mock Jesus to one another and to the scribes. They have achieved Jesus' death, and now they gloat to each other over their victory. Their reference to saving others probably refers to those Jesus healed. They do not understand why He cannot save himself. They do not understand that if he were to save himself, then all people would die in their sins. It is again ironic that they address Jesus correctly as Christ and King, even though they are doing it contemptuously. It is clear that Jesus is being crucified because of His claim to Messiahship. The Jewish leaders in mocking fashion say that they would believe if they saw Jesus come down from the cross, but as Jesus said earlier, "If someone even would come back from the dead, they would not believe" (Luke 16:31, A.T.). The two robbers join in the ridicule.

The true nature and purpose of Jesus' mission was to die on behalf of many; therefore, He cannot come down from the cross if He is to carry out His mission as the obedient Son. He cannot save others if He saves himself. The chief priests miss the whole point of Jesus' mission as Messiah (Christ) and as king. He must stay on the cross in order to accomplish His mission. The Messiah is not a conquering king like David who will rid the land of Romans. The real Messiah is the suffering servant who comes to lay down His life for the sheep. The learners of Jesus did not really understand this idea, and the chief priests did not understand it either. Mark writes his book to his church so that they will understand Jesus' true mission. This is also the point of the book of Mark for us. Jesus was the suffering servant who came to give His life on behalf of our sins that we may live. Jesus' kingship and Messiahship were not what the Jews had expected, nor is it what Mark's Gentile readers would have expected. Jesus is both Lord and Christ because He fulfilled God's will for His life through suffering and dying.

Some people today neglect the nature and purpose of Jesus' mission to all people and concentrate on other worthy projects that select a certain few. It was not only for the poor and minorities that Jesus died on the cross, but for all people. This does not mean the church can ignore the poor and minorities, but the church must serve all people as Christ did, even to the giving of its life for their salvation.

The person who reads this section, which is so brutal to Jesus, cannot help but remember "the rest of the story," that is, His resurrection. Paul's hymn in Philippians 2:5-11 vividly illustrates not just the humiliation of Jesus that we see in this section, but also God's exaltation of Jesus. He is exalted because He is obedient. This is another powerful lesson for Mark's readers and for us. Obedience to God, even in times of great suffering and humiliation, will bring God's ultimate approval.

Mark continues his time keeping by remarking that darkness was over the land from the sixth to the ninth hour (Mark 15:33). Why the darkness occurs we do not know, but it seems to be a sign of the significance of Jesus' crucifixion. In the Old Testament, darkness is a sign both of catastrophe and of God's wrath. Note, for example, the darkness that preceded the killing of the first-born in Egypt at the Passover (Exodus 10:21—11:10).

Jesus' cry, "My God, My God, why have you abandoned me?" has been variously interpreted. Some say that Jesus' cry is triumphant since it is a quotation from Psalm 22:1. Quoting the first verse of the Psalm is equivalent to quoting the whole, and since the whole psalm ends in the triumph of the righteous, Jesus' cry is not a cry of desperation but of triumph. Others would say that Jesus only felt deserted but in reality He was not. The traditional interpretation that God in fact turned away from Jesus when Jesus became the sacrifice for our sin is the clearest meaning. We can better understand the horribleness of sin when we see God's having to turn away from His only-born Son because, as Paul expresses it in 2 Corinthians 5:21, "The one not knowing sin, He [God] made *sin* in order that we might become the rightness of God in him [Christ]" (A.T.). Even in the cry of desperation, Jesus expresses His personal relationship by crying out, "My God." Jesus had a premonition of this desertion and humiliating death when He was in Gethsemane, and that is the reason for His prayer that perhaps there might be another way.

Because Jesus' cry began in Hebrew, the term for "my God" *(Eli)* sounded like the word *Elijah* to those close by. The idea of the coming of Elijah before the Messianic age was well known, but Mark has already shown that Elijah came as a forerunner in

John, and that John was violently received and killed just as Jesus is. The crowd, thinking they hear a cry for Elijah, wants to see whether Elijah will really come. They offer Jesus a sponge with vinegar (really a sour wine common among peasants) in order to quench His thirst and keep Him alive to see whether Elijah will come. We can presume that Jesus did not drink this wine either.

Jesus breathes His last breath, shouts, and dies (Mark 15:37). The verb here is best translated very literally as "expired," that is, "breathed out."

Mark notes two immediate results of Jesus' death. First, the temple curtain is torn from the top down to the bottom into two pieces. Because this event is a public demonstration similar to the darkness, which shows God's disapproval and rejection, we must assume that the curtain mentioned is the one in front of the Holy Place. That curtain could be seen by anyone coming into the temple court area. It is also true for Mark and his audience that the splitting of the temple curtain was a sign of the ultimate end of the temple. Perhaps this event carries out the accusation against Jesus that Jesus would destroy the temple and in three days rebuild it, although Jesus himself was referring to His own body.

The second result of Jesus' death is the centurion's exclamation. The centurion, who commanded at least 100 men, had seen the manner in which Jesus died and declared, "Surely this man was the Son of God" (Mark 15:39). Jesus' manner of death shows to this Gentile, a Roman, that Jesus really is the Son of God. The centurion is the only man in Mark's book to make this declaration. To this point, only God and the demons have acknowledged Jesus' Sonship. Everyone has expected the Son of God to come in political power and glory, not to die on a cross. Mark's book is written to show that the true Son of God is exalted especially in death by crucifixion, and it is remarkable that the only person to understand this is a Roman, just like Mark's readers.

Jesus as the Son of God is the key point in Mark's book. Just as Peter's confession that Jesus is the Christ in Mark 8:29 marks the center and turning point of the book, the centurion's exclamation marks the end of the book. Mark began his book with the statement that Jesus was the Christ, the Son of God; he notes Peter's Messianic statement in the middle of the book; and he records the centurion's Son-of-God statement to conclude the book. Mark's purpose was to show that the true nature of Jesus' mission was to demonstrate that the Messiah was the Son of God. Jesus' mission did not mean having earthly power and authority, but it meant His suffering and the sacrifice of His life. Jesus was the suffering servant; Jesus was the obedient Son. Jesus, through giving His life, demonstrated the real nature and purpose of His Messiahship.

Although this passage is the climactic end of the story of Jesus' nature and purpose, it does not conclude the good news, which must also include Jesus' burial and resurrection. These last two events are chronicled with Mark's natural brevity, but he probably also wants to indicate that he has already achieved his main purpose for writing: to show that Jesus is the Christ, the Son of God.

Jesus died utterly alone. Mark indicates that no one is sympathetic to Jesus until after His death. After His death, Mark tells about the exclamation of the centurion. He notes that there are women standing by and that Joseph of Arimathea devotedly buries Jesus.

The three women mentioned in verses 40 and 41 are eyewitnesses to Jesus' death, eyewitnesses to His burial (Mark 15:47), and eyewitnesses to the empty tomb (Mark 16:1ff). There were other women also at the crucifixion who were Jesus' followers and had traveled with Him to Jerusalem. Because Jewish law did not recognize the testimony of women as valid, it is especially significant that Mark cites these women as the only ones who are witnesses of Jesus' death, burial, and resurrection. These three events are the foundation for the good news as Paul expressed it in 1 Corinthians 15:3f.

The Burial (15:42-47)

This is a simple and uncomplicated account, although the reasons for some of the actions are more fully explained in the other Gospels. Since the Sabbath begins at nightfall, it was not Jewish custom to leave a corpse hanging on a cross overnight since hanging on a tree (cross) meant to be cursed by God (Deuteronomy 21:22, 23) and if a corpse was left hanging overnight, the curse extended to the land. Joseph of Arimathea decided to bury Jesus if he could obtain permission. Joseph was a respected member of the Sanhedrin, the group that had condemned Jesus for blasphemy. Either Joseph had kept silent during the trial—perhaps he was not present—or he was overruled. Joseph's wealth is indicated by the tomb where he buried Jesus, by his linen purchase, and the fact that he must have had servants to help him with the tasks. Mark also describes Joseph as one who expected the kingdom of God (Mark 15:43). According to the other Gospels, he was also a secret follower of Jesus.

The body of a crucified person was normally left on the cross for some time. This was especially true for one convicted of treason since the public execution was meant to be a visual deterrent to crime. The family could not claim the body. The lack of a decent burial was a part of the humiliation for treason and crucifixion. The judge, however, could allow burial, but official mourning was prohibited. Mark says that Joseph dared to go to Pilate. Joseph was at risk to approach Pilate. It meant that he had at least a nominal association with Jesus. Pilate was lenient in this case, perhaps because he knew Jesus was really not a traitor. Pilate granted the corpse to Joseph, but only after he made sure that Jesus was really dead. The fact that Jesus was dead in such a short time was a surprise to Pilate; so he needed assurance.

The burial was simple and was done hastily in order that it would be accomplished before nightfall, since no work was allowed on the Sabbath. Having purchased a linen cloth, Joseph had Jesus' body washed and then rolled in the cloth. The unused tomb must have been close by and owned by Joseph. The allusion to the richness of the tomb is a fulfillment of another part of the suffering servant chapter of Isaiah 53.

The tomb was cut into the rock and its entrance was sealed with a large stone. Mark describes the closing of the tomb when he says that Joseph rolled a stone against the door of the tomb. The stone must have been very large to have blocked the door and must have been hewn in a round fashion so that it could be rolled. Normally, the stone was rolled into a ditch in front of the tomb. It would be fairly easy to roll the stone into the ditch, but very difficult to roll it out. The women were aware of this fact when they went on the first day of the week to finish properly burying Jesus' body.

The Empty Tomb (16:1-8)

As mentioned earlier, the women are the witnesses to the death, burial, and resurrection of Jesus. This is true despite Jewish teaching that does not allow a women's testimony as admissible in a court of law. That every Gospel account gives the women precedence in the resurrection stories is a demonstration of the truthfulness of the accounts. If the accounts had been fabricated or harmonized with one another, Peter and the learners would probably have been the first ones to visit the tomb and the first persons to have Jesus appear to them.

The three women come very early, at the rising of the sun, to bring spices to perfume the body of Jesus. Jews did not practice embalming, but did perfume the body as a way of honoring the individual. The women talked about how the large stone could be moved so they would have access to the body. It is clear from their action and conversation that they expect Jesus to be in the tomb. They do not expect an empty tomb.

When the women arrive, the entrance stone has already been rolled back. When they enter the tomb, they see a young man dressed in white clothes sitting on the right side of the tomb. Matthew confirms that the young man is an angel. The Greek word most often translated "angel" is better translated "messenger," and that is really the purpose of this young man. His white clothing is symbolic of his Heavenly source. The women are terrified, but the messenger tells them not to be terrified. This word was also used by Mark in 14:33 to describe Jesus' reaction in Gethsemane as He was contemplating what lay ahead of Him in terms of the cross.

The messenger is aware that the women are seeking Jesus, whom the young man describes as the crucified Nazarene, that is, that they are looking for a corpse. The young man's message is simple and clear: "He has been raised. He is not here. Look! the place where they set Him" (Mark 16:6, A.T.). God's role is still evident because Jesus did not raise himself: God was the one who raised Him. It is God's way of vindicating His Son.

Mark's emphasis appears to be on the empty tomb. The messenger asks the women to examine the place where Jesus had been placed so that they can be convinced that the tomb is empty. There is no actual account of the resurrection by anyone. Resurrection is not proved; it is to be received by trust. There is evidence for resurrection, but it is not conclusive because resurrection is not a normal historical event. The empty tomb is an historical fact. Most attempts to deny the resurrection are attempts at explaining the empty tomb. Some have attempted to explain the empty tomb by saying that Jesus had not really died; others have explained the empty tomb with the idea that someone had stolen the body. The fact of the empty tomb and the appearances of Jesus to several people demonstrated that Jesus was alive after being crucified.

The empty tomb needs God's interpretive Word to explain its meaning. Without it, the death of Jesus on the cross could be taken simply as the death of a person. But God's Word interprets it: He died "for our sins." The empty tomb is simply an empty tomb without God's interpretive Word given through His messenger: "He has been raised; He is not here; Come see the place where they set Him."

The strongest evidence of the empty tomb and Jesus' resurrection is the change in the learners of Jesus and the establishment of the early church. If there had been no resurrection, it is incredible to believe that the learners of Jesus who had fled in fear, and led by Peter who had denied Jesus, could some fifty days later face the same Jews from whom they had fled and accuse them of murdering Jesus. The first proclamation by Peter on Pentecost and all his subsequent proclamations had the resurrection at the core. The empty tomb and the resurrection are the only sufficient way to explain the learners' behavior and the subsequent rise and rapid spread of the early church. Jesus' followers need no longer be afraid of death. Their leader the Messiah died but was resurrected.

The messenger's final words to the women are a form of commission. The women are to go and to tell Jesus' learners and Peter that Jesus is going before them into Galilee, and there the learners will see Him. This is first of all a message of forgiveness. The fact that Peter is mentioned separately is a special note to Peter, who had so vociferously denied Jesus. The learners had all fled, but here Jesus tells them through the messenger and the women that they are still His followers. He wants them to follow Him to Galilee. The message is also a gentle but firm reminder that Jesus had already told them that after He was raised, He would go before them into Galilee (Mark 14:28).

The reaction of the women to the empty tomb and the messenger's words includes fear, trembling, and astonishment. This reaction is demonstrated by their fleeing from the tomb and not telling anyone what they have seen or heard. Fear, trembling, and astonishment are typical reactions that are recorded earlier in Mark when people see the power of God. (Note the astonishment when the paralyzed person is healed in Mark 2:12, the fear and trembling when the woman with a hemorrhage returns to Jesus in Mark 5:33, the great fear when the learners see the wind and waves obey Jesus in Mark 4:41, the herdsmen's flight when their pigs are destroyed in Mark 5:14, the fearful silence of the inner three when they witness the transfiguration in Mark 9:6, and the learners' lack of understanding, their fear, and their amazement as Jesus predicts His death, burial, and resurrection in Mark 9:32 and 10:32). Thus flight, fear, silence, trembling, and astonishment are all earlier reactions to the power and teaching of Jesus. Therefore, we are not surprised at these same reactions by these women.

Why does Mark say that the women did not tell anyone anything? We know from the other Gospel accounts that, in fact, they did report the news eventually to the learners. Historically, they probably were amazed into silence for a short period of time. As was mentioned earlier, this is a typical reaction to divine revelation. But even if that is the case, is that a good way to end the good news book of Mark?

Other Endings to Mark's Gospel (16:9-20)

Ancient manuscripts show us four different endings to Mark's book. The fact that there are four different endings shows us the confusion apparently caused by the abrupt ending at verse 8. Either a portion of the original manuscript was lost (which I think is very unlikely) or Mark really intended to end his book at verse 8.

The traditional ending with verses 9-20 is old, probably written in the second century, but its vocabulary and writing style are not Markan. The material in verses 9-20 is contained more completely in all the other Gospels with the exception of the "signs following" the teaching (Mark 16:17, 18). What is missing from verses 9-20, if it were really by Mark, is the women's report to the learners and the appearance in Galilee, both of which are referenced in verse 7.

Another old ending for Mark contains two verses that mention the women's telling Peter about the resurrection and also mentions Jesus' sending out His learners with the message of eternal salvation. This old ending is clearly compiled to complete what some people thought to be an incomplete ending to Mark's book. Another ending in some manuscripts contains both the endings just discussed.

Mark has a literary reason for ending his book in this peculiar way. Jesus had often urged those whom He healed and the demons to be silent during His ministry. This silence was for various reasons already discussed, but it was for appropriate reasons at the time. The readers of the book have followed the ministry of Jesus through all the healings, through miracles, through the lack of understanding on the part of the learners, and even through the suffering of Jesus when He is forsaken by all His followers. Silence was appropriate during His ministry because Jesus asked for it. But silence is not appropriate now because God's messenger says, "Go, tell." Mark's audience is challenged to do what the women do not. Mark's audience is challenged to go and tell. Astonishment is certainly an appropriate reaction as one reads slowly and completely through Mark's book, but that astonishment should not paralyze the reader. On the contrary, it should energize us to go and to tell. We need to read Mark's book carefully so that we can catch that initial amazement.

The ending at verse 8 is consistent with Mark's purpose in writing the book, which was to show that Jesus is the Christ, the Son of God by His life and death. No one trusted Jesus during His life, and even the women remained silent, but Mark's readers know otherwise. Therefore, they are not to be like the learners or the women. The readers are to go and to proclaim that Jesus is the Christ, the Son of God. You and I are the current readers of Mark's book. You and I know better also, and therefore, we are also to go and to proclaim, "Jesus is the Christ, the Son of God."

SUGGESTED READING

The following volumes on Mark have been consulted by the writer and are recommended for further study.

Achtemeier, P. J. *Mark*. Philadelphia: Fortress, 1975.

Anderson, H. *The Gospel of Mark*. Grand Rapids: Eerdmans, 1981.

Bratcher, R. G. *A Translator's Guide to the Gospel of Mark*. New York: United Bible Societies, 1981.

Bratcher, R. B. and E. A. Nida. *A Translator's Handbook on the Gospel of Mark*. New York: United Bible Societies, 1961.

Cranfield, C. E. B. *The Gospel According to Saint Mark*. Cambridge: Cambridge University, 1977.

Hurtado, L. W. *Mark*. San Francisco: Harper and Row, 1983.

Lane, W. L. *The Gospel According to Mark*. Grand Rapids: Eerdmans, 1974.

Mann, C. S. *Mark*. Garden City, N.Y.: Doubleday, 1986.

Rhodes, D. M. and D. M. Michie. *Mark as Story*. Philadelphia: Fortress, 1982.

Schweizer, E. *The Good News According to Mark*. Richmond: John Knox, 1970.